THIS

FIERY

LOVE

THIS
FIERY LOVE

Fanning the
Original Flame

BY

Janice Leasure Woodrum

PREPARING THE WAY
PUBLISHERS

PREPARING THE WAY

PUBLISHERS

411 Zandecki Rd.
Chehalis, WA. 98532

Janice Leasure Woodrum

THIS FIERY LOVE
Fanning the Original Flame

ISBN 13: 978-0615449623 ISBN 10: 061544962x

DEDICATION

This book is dedicated to Kit Carson Leasure Jr. and Irene Elizabeth Day Leasure, my parents. They were my best examples of "fiery love," as seen in their day-to-day life in the small home they shared with my two older sisters and me near a small rural Kansas town. Dad was a welder of aircraft parts for Boeing Company in Wichita, Kansas during part of the Second World War, and Mother was a school teacher. When my Grandfather in eastern Kansas became disabled, they moved back to the farm where he had been farming. It was the land homesteaded by my Great-Grandfather Zebediah Leasure in 1855, and which he farmed surrounding his service as an officer in the Civil War, fought only a few miles away near the Kansas-Missouri border.

Dad and Mom demonstrated to me a living picture of the "fiery love" that is the theme of this small book. They exemplified for better or worse, richer or poorer, in sickness or in health, to love and to cherish 'til death... One of my fondest memories of them is of the early morning discussions they had day after day and year after year. In our small country house, the kitchen door was very near to my bedroom door, and their conversation was a dull hum in my ears as I awoke early every morning to prepare for school. I couldn't make out the words, but early morning by morning they would always be there in the kitchen sketching out the days' events

5

over coffee, and solving the daily situations awaiting them in the management of the farm and family. Harsh or angry words were almost never heard between them, and we never questioned their deep enjoyment of each other, and their appreciation of the partnership they shared in marriage, faith, work, play and parenthood.

This obvious and unquestionable quality of love exemplified for me over many years became undoubtedly the model for the kind of love that I wanted to experience someday with my own "prince charming," and which I indeed am so thankful to enjoy with him to this day.

I praise God for the heritage of the many rich memories, from attending the small country church together; to the summer vacations when we escaped the farm chores to camp in Colorado or beyond; to the many high school games, music contests and school plays they never failed to attend. In sharing some of the attributes of this love, as well as other life experiences and truths from the love manual, the Word of God, I hope to enrich the vocabulary of our "love language" for our current marriages, or perhaps the marriages you have yet to embark upon. My experience has convinced me entirely that the environment of love we provide for our families, and model for those observing us, can be the quality and intensity of love they will seek to develop within their own marriages. Fiery love catches fire in others!

TABLE OF CONTENTS

PROLOGUE

"Place me like a seal over your heart, like a seal on your arm; for love is as strong as death ... it burns like blazing fire, like a mighty flame. Many waters cannot quench love..." Song of Songs 8:6-7

Most of us who are married can at least vaguely remember our wedding day. We woke with that jittery feeling in our stomachs – a sign of eager anticipation, perhaps mixed with a touch of fear, or at the very least the sobering realization that this was a very serious step. It was a step designed to last a lifetime of ups and downs, days of richer or poorer, moments of sickness and health ... 'til death do us part. It was a sobering moment indeed.

But we were in love, and that made all the difference. Or if you're in an Eastern culture, perhaps you weren't so much in love, as this was a marriage arranged by the elders of your families. But there was an anticipation of love that would grow as you grew to know and appreciate each other over time.

Song of Songs, the "love book" of the Bible says love burns like a blazing fire; many waters cannot quench love. Indeed the love of a man and woman for each other must be one of the strongest forces available to mankind. And I believe a love that "burns like blazing fire" is a primary goal and treasure of most persons choosing to "tie the knot" of marriage together.

But with the passing of subsequent years of life together ... the birth of children, the difficult times of meager finances, sickness, changing jobs and locations, and other inevitable events of married life, the "many waters" seem to do their best to extinguish that blazing fire of the original love, or at the very least tone it down to a flickering candle light.

This author has discovered over several decades of married life, that the original flame can indeed be fed with new kindling and fanned with the wind of the Holy Spirit, so that it not only ceases to die down; it is instead nurtured into a "blazing fire" of love again between you and your mate. This book will share some foundational truths of the Scriptures, and also some anecdotes of personal experience. These will back up very strong and sincere convictions and a wealth of hope that your fire can blaze again with rekindled admiration, respect and true love.

Here's a toast to your "blazing fire" to be!

INTRODUCTION

As I write the first words on a brand new ring binder, the green cover I have chosen seems to beckon to me. There is a pile of these binders on the shelf in our store room – picked up several months ago when school started, and they were reduced to 15 cents each. Why did I choose this one, amidst a broad palette of bright colors? It's not even a forest tree green, but an off-green, a little lighter and yellower, like the very first shoots of my pea plants in my garden this spring. Guess it just seemed to say to me, "Choose me – I'm new!"

It was a fitting choice for the first draft of a brand new book ... a book that will reflect a life so rich, so vivid and so full of "new" ... new surprises, new places, new faces, new adventures, and newness of love.

An old song is reflecting on the mirror of my heart from decades past:

"The steadfast love of the Lord never ceases; His mercies never come to an end. They are new every morning, new every morning; great is your faithfulness oh Lord. Great is Your faithfulness!"

My heart says, "I'm counting on it Lord, today as always to be true." For the worn brown easy chair just a few feet away from my feet in my matching worn brown easy chair is empty today. It's always full first thing in the morning ... full of smiles and the aroma of a fresh hot cup of coffee. It's full of words expressing wonder at a long forgotten but newly discovered scripture, a new spiritual insight, a new idea birthed out of it, and a new eagerness to approach the dawn together to answer each other with the well-worn question: "What's God saying to us today?"

It's the common first question we utter in our pre-dawn, get your eyes fully open moments. For you see, God so often speaks to one of us even before we speak to each other. One may awaken with a song "playing" in the gooey gray matter somewhere deep in the miracle of brain and mind He fashioned for the first man so many centuries ago from that soft clay of the "garden." It was the first garden, crafted with such great beauty and personality – filled with creatures of every kind and just waiting for the first Adam to wake up under God's first kiss and see them – soon to name them.

The warm body squeezed snugly in the space next to me in my old easy chair lets out a big sigh, as if to add his vote of agreement. For I believe dogs were made for the special assignments God would present for them to love and befriend man as no other creature could or would (Cat lovers, please bear with me). Things like aiding the blind safely across streets with traffic, helping firemen discover and drag out unconscious forms from burning buildings, aiding rescue workers in locating the owner of the T-shirt imprinted with the scent of the three year old who wandered off from the picnic, or smelling urine to help researchers diagnose prostate cancer. But best of all is fulfilling the highest destiny – that is being "man's best friend," especially when the man's (or woman's) best friend isn't in the nearby chair where they always are at 6 am. every day, morning by morning.

"One bite for me and one for you," my actions say to my little Shi-Tzu partner squeezed in beside me, eyeing my breakfast roll expectantly. But still his deep brown eyes ask me disquietedly, "But where *is* he?"

He recognizes better than anyone (unless it's the golden retriever asleep at his guard on the floor next to my chair) that "the chair," Daddy's chair is empty today – empty for the first time in

13

months of mornings of the marvelous repetitive routine. For rising early to answer the question, "What's God saying to us today?" has been our practice from the first morning we awoke together as husband and wife so many years ago. He knows only that one's absence could keep us from this secret place, found in the garden in the sweet pre-dawn stillness we share together.

Yes, Daddy's gone today, high above the Pacific Ocean, to arrive in India after 20+ more hours of air flight, changing planes several times, and finding comfort and inspiration inside the "partner book" to the one on my chair-side table which beckons me to answer the question, "What's God saying today?"

And he'll go from India to Burma (now Myanmar) and on to the Philippines, returning to his brown chair in a month, by God's grace. His job as a seasoned missionary on this trip is primarily to meet with weary leaders in these countries, refueling and refreshing their hearts with answers to the question common to God's children of any color, "What's God saying?"

The pages you've already read of this introduction answer in part the question for today. God is saying, "Write it down." My mind takes a brief detour excursion back to the airport gate yesterday evening, where we had our last passionate kisses in the corner of the waiting room, our last endearing words and our tears of pain in parting for these four weeks ahead of us.

After he passed through the electronic metal-detecting arch and moved on toward his gate, I stood behind following his form as he grew smaller and smaller. Then suddenly he turned and his eyes found me watching him. He put down his carry-on bag and lifted his arms towards me with a bellowing "I LOVE YOU!!!" that echoed in that cavernous departure hall of the airport. I echoed back in a voice not nearly so strong as his, "I love you!" Then with more glances, waves and kisses thrown, until he was entirely out of sight, we completed the ritual mating pattern of mammals uniquely designed for each other ... and then he was gone.

It's this love – this passionate, fiery, exciting, sustaining, enduring love – that God is saying I should begin to write down in these days of almost agonizing stillness. So still I can hear the breathing of both our dogs nearby.

A week or so ago, Dave and I agreed I should begin another book, and somehow between the two of us we retrieved the "T's" of these chapter titles from out of our volumes of experiences together over the years.

This deeply satisfying, sustaining love issues forth from our times in these two old brown chairs very early in the morning, every day with our Lord, and from the moment-by-moment experiences of our fiery love together in the hours of each day thereafter.

And even late last evening in his layover at the San Francisco airport, he spoke to me while waiting for his trans-Pacific flight. Together we agreed on some verses I could share in each chapter to enhance each one with a touch from God's enduring hearth, the hearth that springs out of His heart.

For God's torch, and His ways revealed in the pages of scripture are what make a book like this even worth reading. What is the kindling for the fire of our passionate "love affair" with each other?

What are the logs that fuel it through the days? And what sustains the enduring glow of embers even when the logs are pulled apart? Perhaps they're not so much "secrets hidden," as they are "patterns forgotten" that need only to be brought up and stirred up again to bring that waning glow of embers into a blazing warmth of "fiery love."

Pull up a comfy old chair and share some moments with us; perhaps we can watch God breathe new flames into your love as God wrote in the Song of Songs, *"It burns like blazing fire."*

18

Chapter 1

~ TORCH ~

"Place me like a seal over your heart, like a seal on your arm; for love is as strong as death; its jealousy unyielding as the grave. It burns like blazing fire, like a mighty flame. Many waters cannot quench love; rivers cannot wash it away."

Song of Songs 8: 6-7a

The margin of my Bible contains a statement regarding these three sentences as follows: **"These three wisdom statements characterize marital love as the strongest, most unyielding and invincible force in human experience."**

I was nearly "blown away" with the impact of these statements. And I was almost immediately reminded by the Holy Spirit of a verse in Ephesians 5:25, *"Husbands, love your wives, just as Christ loved the Church and gave Himself up for her to make her holy..."*

In this verse we glimpse likewise the strongest, most unyielding and invincible force in human (the God-man Jesus') experience, as

He is the model for Christian husbands to follow.

Here we see, within these verses the power source behind the requirements for husbands found in Ephesians 5:25. It is that same power that caused Jesus to yield in the garden to the inevitable hideous suffering of the cross; the power that carried Him through the excruciating pain and agony of suffering for our sins; and the power that raised Him up from death and the grave to seat Him with the Father in the highest place (Ephesians 1:20-21).

This blazing fire of unquenchable love described in Song of Songs chapter eight nearly a thousand years earlier, is revealed in Ephesians to be the self-sacrificing, unyielding flame of love demonstrated by Jesus on the cross about AD 33. This author of love, our Lord Jesus, is the source of our marital love which is said to be "the most invincible force in human experience" today.

Faith should rise up in our hearts that within Jesus' finished work lies the secret formula and power for our marital love to be rekindled into a blazing fire, then fanned continuously to be a strong and sure torch-light for our families and others.

The torch of Jesus' fiery love demonstrated for us is the foundation upon which the tower of T's of this book will be built and established.

On the flip side, we will also identify torches of our own imagination, our own appetites, our own zeal and our own aspirations that may be quenching or overpowering the flame of love in our marriages.

Isaiah 50:10-11 advises, *"Who among you fears the Lord and obeys the word of His servant? Let him who walks in the dark, who has no light, trust in the name of the Lord and rely on his God. But now, all you who light fires and provide yourselves with flaming torches, go walk in the light of your fires and of the torches you have set ablaze. This is what you shall receive from my hand; you will lie down in torment."*

These verses spell out a rather vivid picture of the demise that can result when we light the torches of our own ambitions and our own resources, rather than seeking God's best goals for our lives and His resources to accomplish them. Now as we continue to consider some other "T" subjects that relate to marital joy and harmony, we pray for grace to fear the Lord, and to obey and walk in the light of His Word, trusting in the name of the Lord Jesus Christ. Amen.

Chapter 2

~ TEAM ~

As I consider the word "team" I am reminded of last Saturday's game. Our grandsons Ben and Brennan, ages 10 and 8, had their last game of the football season for this year. Having been to several of their games over these past two months, we could see a marked improvement in their skills in this game.

We could see increments of improvement in the team members' skills in keeping their eyes on the ball, passing the ball with accuracy, running the ball, depending on the unique skills and talents of each other, and in other words – embracing the concepts of unity and pride in working as a team. As a result they actually won the game, and quite significantly! It left a nice "taste in their mouths" – a good ending to a rather poor overall season.

On the other hand, big brother Brady (13) on the Jr. High team had a stellar season, winning all of their games and finishing undefeated! As we watched and mentally compared his team's performance with the younger brothers' team, the level of inter-dependency, recognition of unique skills of team members, communication patterns, and teamwork of this older team were all markedly advanced from those of the younger team. I pondered the question, "What was the key to their success?"

As we talked with our son and his wife (the players' parents) the reason for the differences in levels of performance between Brady's team and the younger boys' team quickly became apparent. The reason was because in the older team, these same boys had been playing together for several years ... ever since they were in the same league as the younger boys are playing on now. Over the years, Brady's team had learned a great deal about each others' strengths and weaknesses, communication patterns, favorite plays, endurance levels, etc. The growing together in their discovery of these issues, as well as others, had been the primary element in their record of greater success this year than in the past.

It reminds me of the concept of "team" as it applies to marriage and family. Jesus said in Matthew 19:5-6, *"For this reason a man will leave his father and mother and be united to his wife, and the two will become one flesh. So they are no longer two, but one. Therefore what God has joined together, let man not separate."*

We could probably "camp" on these two verses for several chapters, but to make our point let's just consider this "two become one" as the smallest definition of "team." In the case of my three grandsons, the longer they had played together with a team, the more they functioned in a cooperative and cohesive unit in order to win the game. Likewise, *time* and *practice* became the primary ingredients required to make the team a cohesive and effective unit, prepared to compete effectively against an opposing team.

I'm flashing on a memory from the evening my husband proposed to me. After the romantic and unforgettably meaningful moments and commitments were exchanged, Dave decided he was hungry from the nearly two hour drive from his home some distance away. Eggs, toast and bacon sounded good to the man who only an hour ago had no appetite at all. Wonder why? Go figure!

So after he placed his order, I proceeded to try to prepare his eggs the way he liked them, without becoming queasy in my stomach in the process. You see, my choice of fried eggs has always been one shade harder than translucent, and one degree softer than cardboard. In other words, hard ... VERY HARD! His on the other hand need to be barely congealed on the outside and sickeningly gooey on the inside. I failed to cease cooking them at just the right stage of runny goo, and felt a failure at my first real cooking expedition with my husband-to-be.

So what about his eggs today, many years and many dozen eggs later? As you might expect after many years of practice, my skills are honed, and his eggs are cooked to precisely the stage of un-cooked-ness that he finds tantalizing, while I choke back a stifled gag reflex. Nevertheless, the point is – it's not an issue anymore. He's feeling full and happy; I'm feeling adept and satisfied in my role, and we get on with other "loftier" issues than eggs. Over the years many other differences have similarly worked themselves out in the seasons of living and loving together.

The important take-home prize from this story is: *It takes time and practice to learn to be a team.* Will you practice "taking time" to discover and also put into practice those little things that he/she finds so important in life?

Can you really look and listen to what he/she wants and needs in order to be really happy?

My mind settles for a moment on an incident about a week ago. Dave was preparing to leave in a few days for a month's whirlwind schedule of missionary activities in three Asian countries. So I decided to make him his favorite meal – spaghetti with lots of vegetables in the sauce, just the way he likes it. So I went after all the necessary ingredients and cooked up what I thought was just the right blend of tomato sauce, vegetables and spices, only to discover there were no spaghetti noodles in the cupboard; there were only the wider version that look like spaghetti ironed flat, vermicelli I think. So that's what I served, thinking "a noodle is a noodle" whether round or flat like vermicelli – same exact ingredients, and it should taste just the same. But when I inquired how he liked the special dinner I had made, he said it was delicious ... but with reluctance he shared that he preferred to have spaghetti next time. I said, "What do you mean? I made you spaghetti the way you like it!" (My frustration at having somehow missed the mark was showing.) He said, "No, I mean spaghetti *noodles.*"

So what would I do with that one? Would I maintain the sense of team between us in these last few days together before a month apart, swallowing my pride and gently promising to buy ordinary spaghetti noodles the next time I went to the store? Or would I press the fight to be "right," only to lose the greater battle to maintain unity and love in the loaded and stressful atmosphere of the rapidly expiring last few days before a long and lonely separation?

In earlier days I might have pressed my point that all noodles are created equal and won the argument, only to lose the greater battle for unity and love. But this time, thankfully, I won the battle for unity, love and marital peace, acknowledging his desire for the "round ones next time," and rightly appreciating his comments that the meal was quite delicious apart from his preference in noodles.

It seems in retrospect like a silly and moot point to get rattled over, but it's a good example of a common situation that can keep our marriages in a constant state of marginal disunity, failing to fully come into team in such a way as to win the prize of pleasing God and growing in unity, peace and love in our relationship.

If you're finding that you're not really "connecting" at the heart with your mate these days, perhaps there is some wisdom in the adage, "Don't sweat the small stuff." Start focusing on the important things that make you a team together, learning to give thanks for all the godly traits that you *do* love and appreciate; and focus on the things that drew you together in the first place.

Perhaps it's a good time to examine just a bit more closely what makes up a strong team ...

Time – Energy – Admiration – Memories

TIME: Our grandsons who play football and their parents share a duplex with Dave and me, and it has made me a little weary watching them load up and head for football practice day after day. It has taken a chunk out of most of my daughter-in-law's days the past couple of months, but having played several sports in school years earlier, she recognized that time practicing and playing as a team is vital for connectedness, harmony, skill and success. And she embraces what is required to get the boys to their practices. Why should it be any different in the teamwork of marriage? Time is perhaps the greatest option for investing ourselves in each other. But we'll discuss that thought and examine it more closely in another chapter.

ENERGY: The young football players came home draggin' their tails every day, having expended plenty of energy during the daily practice.

It seems we only have so much energy, and in my 60's I don't quite have the quota I used to have of it. The question is, "How will we spend it?" How will we apportion what we have towards the tasks of life on our plates?

I remember early in my Christian walk when my children were toddlers. I had read the book His Needs, Her Needs and learned that the author had studied large groups of men. The majority of the men studied had expressed a common need in their lives. That is the need for a somewhat peaceful and orderly place to come home to after the stresses of the work day. It made good sense to me, so I made an effort to apply my time and energies in such a way as to accommodate this common preference. With toddlers in the house in a rainy climate (Western Washington, USA), there was quite a mountain of toys strewn in most every room by the end of the day, an empty bottle or Sippy Cup here and there, and on some days even a dirty diaper on the back of the toilet waiting to be washed out (we rarely used disposables back then in the early 70's) – can you imagine it?!

I decided to make a change in the way I expended both my time and energy in those days. If a friend called me late in the afternoon and wanted to visit awhile, I would cut off my conversation in time to make a sweep of the toys strewn around the house and help the toddlers find the places for their toys in their room. Bathrooms were checked; the master bed was made and the room tidied; and dirty dishes were dealt with. And supper was "in process" when hubby walked in the door.

In retrospect I can't thank the author, Dr. Willard Harley, Jr. enough for these very wise words of advice. In choosing to expend my energy in this way, it said to my husband that I wanted to hold up my end of the partnership, creating an atmosphere of peace and orderliness as a solace after a rushed and hectic day of work. It was well worth the energy and has been a lifetime habit that has enhanced mutual respect and partnership in the marriage "team."

This particular scenario may not apply to your situation, but now is a good time to examine the distribution of the time and energy in your life. When it's nearly time for him to return home, have you made the effort to comb your hair and apply a little make-up that you know he likes (not only when you "go out" together)? Are you exchanging the saggy and perhaps somewhat soiled T-shirt for something a little more flattering?

Take some quiet moments with God to consider if some energy and time expenditure adjustments in your life could make a big difference in expressing your love to your mate, paving the way for greater harmony in the home and a blaze in the fire of your love.

You male readers might want to take some moments to consider how a few minutes well spent might speak volumes to your mate. For us gals a funny or romantic card with some "love" words inside can pave the way for a *sweet* evening. Or the glow from a "handful size" bouquet of mixed flowers can stoke the fire of your fellowship together. Use your imagination.

ADMIRATION / APPRECIATION: When marital harmony seems to be waning, these little "A" words are the start towards a rekindled atmosphere of the "fiery love" you'd like to see in the marriage.

Take 5-10 minutes and ask the Lord to remind you of three things:

1. What words have I spoken to my mate to express my admiration or appreciation for anything in the past week? (Write them down if you find any.)
2. What words could I (as a woman) begin to speak, or actions could I do to express the A words for:
   - His work to support the family?
   - His physical appearance and personal hygiene?
   - His attention towards the children?
   - His personality attributes that drew me to him in the first place?
   - His chores done around the house (taking out the trash, etc.)?
   - His expressions of his love and affection?
   - His unique thoughts and ideas?
   - His good, praiseworthy character attributes?

- His walk with the Lord and spiritual leadership of the family?
- Anything else I can discover?
3. Or as a man, what words might I use to express my appreciation to her for:
    - Her efforts to keep the house clean and tidy?
    - Her habit of keeping the refrigerator stocked with the drinks and snacks I enjoy?
    - Her efforts to cook the dishes I like, especially on special occasions?
    - Her patience to listen to my tales of the challenges I'm facing at work?
    - Her seemingly endless trips to run children to practices, lessons, etc.?
    - Her abilities to balance the many varied tasks and schedules in life.
    - Her ways of keeping up her physical appearance.
    - Her patience in dealing with the discipline of the children carefully.

The list could go on and on for both sexes. And of course if both are working outside the home, these sample lists of praiseworthy items could take on very different flavors.

But now that I've jogged your memory a bit, make your own list of what you've discovered. Then make a concerted effort to voice your appreciation or admiration in some way every day. Even keep a record for awhile to be sure you are really living up to your good intentions.

One idea the Lord gave me was really quite easy to do and surely reaped us some great benefits in our love relationship. Dave was working as a designer/builder, and traveled an hour or so to the home he was building with two of our sons. I packed a lunch for him every day.

When I went shopping I tried to pick up a variety of things I could include in his lunch cooler. I kept in stock materials for at least three different kinds of sandwiches, various fruits and raw vegetables, a good assortment of his favorite kinds of cookies (homemade whenever possible), dried fruit or nuts, chips or pretzels, cheese slices, yogurt, snack cakes or pies, a serving of milk and sometimes even a piece of candy.

But that's not what he looked forward to the most. While he was dressing for work I would put his lunch together, and include a love note hastily written on his napkin. It often contained a phrase of scripture, a silly poem or saying, a cute poorly drawn picture, a word of admiration or appreciation, or anything else the Holy Spirit would put on my mind. It was the highlight of his day to take out his lunch and see what kind of silly or serious love note I had included at the top of his lunch. He said the other men on the job would sometimes watch him to see his response to my love notes. If I ever forgot to include one, he didn't fail to draw it to my attention. When I would unpack his empty lunch box in the evening, I would really get "in trouble" if I ever threw one away. He wanted to stack these notes in a pile on the dresser in his closet, and there's a pile of them there even as I sit writing this little story.

Sounds like what school kids would do, you say? Perhaps, but isn't that the point? If my man feels more like a "young" man, it works out all the better for both of us (in several ways)!

For men reading this book, perhaps all you need in order to develop a greater appreciation of your wife's attributes and actions is a day or two walking in her shoes.

A daughter just left after a weekend with me while her husband went elk hunting in our region. The four year old and almost two year old had a lovely and lively time, and now having said "bye bye" to them all, I collapse in a chair and breathe a huge sigh at all the energy and patience it takes to keep up with them, and all the gazillion decisions there are to make for ones this age – from what to feed them, when and how to bring needed correction, how to preserve the eye-balls of my small dog from the probing 1½ year old fingers, and last but not least how to have an even remotely intelligent conversation in the midst of it. I developed a new sense of appreciation for her motherly role! And if the men reading this haven't done so lately, keep the kids for a few hours while Mom goes shopping, and you'll develop a new sense of appreciation for some of the things she does day after day.

Note: If you genuinely can't think of *anything* worthy of voicing appreciation or admiration, perhaps you need more help than this little book can offer. Start with a same-sex elder in your church fellowship who you trust and respect. Begin to discuss your concerns privately with her/him and go from there.

MEMORIES: Memories are like mail … email in particular. Every once in awhile my computer seems to bog down and won't do the work as efficiently as it used to. I have to go through the "in box" and delete some emails I no longer need in order to increase speed and efficiency.

When our marriage relationship seems to "bog down" perhaps we need to look at the "in box" of our memories and thought processes. Are there things we need to process through and delete? For instance, what do you do with the memory of that time when the kids were sick and she forgot to take your suit to the dry cleaners before your trip out of town. Or the time he forgot and scheduled an important business meeting on your birthday weekend.

You know in your heart you've carried these old wounds too long, and you've even pulled them out of the garbage can and into the current conversation more than once over the years, just to put an exclamation point onto the current marital disagreement you're dealing with. If so, then it's time to "delete" these memories from your "in box" before they bog down your systems together to a near halt.

What's that you're saying? You can't find the "delete" button. Let me help you. It's mentioned several times in different ways in the "operation manual" for your marriage. Here's one that works well if you try it.

"Therefore as God's chosen people, holy and dearly loved, clothe yourselves with compassion, kindness, humility, gentleness and patience. Bear with each other and forgive whatever grievances you may have against one another. Forgive as the Lord forgave you. And over all these virtues put on love, which binds them all together in perfect unity."

Colossians 3:12-13

Sometimes in my work I run into a task on my computer that I just can't handle with my level of technical savvy. So I call in my husband or a daughter to help me, before I waste a lot of time hitting a dead-end.

Likewise, we have a helper we can call in when the "forgive" and "forget" functions are just beyond our level of expertise. Here it is:

"In the same way, the Spirit helps us in our weaknesses. We do not know what we ought to pray for, but the Spirit Himself intercedes for us with groans that words cannot express. And He who searches our hearts knows the mind of the spirit, because the Spirit intercedes for the saints in accordance with God's will."

Romans 8:26-27

"Holy Spirit, I need your help to begin to forgive and forget the wounds and disappointments of the past that keep me from experiencing the love and fullness of joy you have for me in my marriage and my other relationships. Come and clean house in my heart and mind. Make me willing to forgive and forget, so we can experience all you have for us in this marriage and in our entire family.

In Jesus' Name, Amen"

There's one last function we shouldn't neglect before we move away from the email of our memories. It is the column on the left and it says "SAVE." The Holy Spirit is a genius at this function, and He can easily highlight, italicize and capitalize those memory messages worth keeping and even magnifying. Let's refresh our memory on how that function works.

"Finally, brothers (and sisters) whatever is true, whatever is noble, whatever is right, whatever is pure, whatever is lovely, whatever is admirable – if anything is excellent or praiseworthy – think about such things ... and the God of peace will be with you."

Philippians 4:8-9

When you take a little time to put these verses into practice, you'll find the good memories, personality traits, and natural strengths of your spouse are being recognized and magnified in your field of vision. And remember also Psalm 34:3: *"Oh magnify the Lord with me, and let us exalt His name together."* (NKJV)

When we magnify Him in praise and worship, our own challenges and troubles get smaller as He appears larger in our frame of vision. Thank Him for what is good; praise Him for His faithfulness to date; and worship Him in His almighty power, holiness and His endless compassion. He becomes in our thinking large enough and powerful enough to help us solve our problems and strengthen our marriages.

In Matthew 11:28-30 Jesus said, *"Come to me, all you who are weary and burdened, and I will give you rest. Take my yoke upon you and learn from me, for I am gentle and humble in heart, and you will find rest for your souls. For my yoke is easy and my burden is light."*

Picture yourself with your mate as oxen in a field wearing a common yoke and pulling a heavy implement such as a plow or a wagon. The yoke has been chafing and you're having trouble continuing on. Why don't you invite Jesus to come into the center of your yoke, so He can pull with you moment by moment and day by day; His shoulders are big, and you'll find He can help you pull the load more easily and more effectively if you let Him. Take a moment to pray together if you can, and invite Him into the center of your yoke, pulling with you through both the easy and the more difficult terrains of life. He is faithful and strong when we are wounded or weak.

I have one last thought on the subject of "yoke." Second Corinthians 6:14 says, *"Do not be yoked together with unbelievers."* The King James Version reads: *"Be ye not unequally yoked together."*

I've seen people who are dating set themselves up for a failed marriage as they ignore or neglect this word. Perhaps they have many things in common and they really are "in love." But if they are not equally yoked, inevitably friction will weaken and perhaps break the bonds of marriage at some later date.

The advice of this scripture can go even deeper than that. It applies to more than simply marrying another Christian. Over the years we have known many couples who are both confessing Christians. But one barely has his foot over the "starting line" while the other is filled with zeal for the Lord and racing forward. With the former, the stronger partner has to beg and plead to get his partner to the church service several times a month, where the one with more zeal for Christ wants to be there on Sunday, and a mid-week Bible Study or home group as well – maybe even dreaming of a short term mission experience. One wants to pray and read the Bible together, and the other never can find the time. This spiritual tension, over time, can place serious hazards in the path of this couple.

So in our opinion "equally yoked" can also mean letting God lead you who are single to the mate with a similar zeal that you have for Christ and the Church, and this will lead to the most satisfying and fruitful life together in Christ for the long haul.

Chapter 3

~ TIME ~

We already discussed "time" briefly in reference to the "T" of team, but now let's borrow a few moments from our daily allotment to discuss it more fully.

First I challenge you to take a quick inventory of the time you and your spouse are together routinely in the presence of your children or other persons in an average day or week (outside of your workplace). Make a written note of your estimate. Then make a second estimate of how much non-sleeping "alone" time you have with your mate.

Now remember back to your dating days when you could hardly wait to spend time alone together. You were discovering new things about each other, and seeking to please each other. You hung onto his or her words as well as to his/her hands. Next consider: Are the hours you spent then in an average "date night" greater than your "alone together" time now in an average week? If so, don't be surprised if your marital joy and intimacy is sadly waning. So is my philodendron plant in the guest bedroom that I haven't watered in about two weeks.

Perhaps you've had so little alone time recently, you don't even know your spouse today as well as you did some time ago. A few weeks ago Dave and I took time to do the following exercise together. We decided to take 5 minutes to write down in private our favorite in each of the following categories:

Food	Color
Animal	Book of the Bible
Book	Drink
Movie	Dessert
Song	Vegetable

Then we took another 5 minutes to do the same thing, only answering how we thought our spouse would answer.

After that we took the next 45 minutes or so comparing our lists for how we rated ourselves and each other.

We had a ball doing this exercise! We were surprised in many areas, and kicked ourselves for not knowing what was clearly each one's favorite. But the real surprise that kicked us in the pants was this:

I would read the favorite I had listed for myself in a category, and he would say, "But you know your favorite is _____." And you know what? HE WAS RIGHT!!! What he listed for my favorite was actually more clearly my favorite than what I had listed! And the same thing was true when we went over his list. This happened two or three times. We were truly amazed to see that in several categories, we knew our mate's answer better than he/she did! We really had a good laugh over that totally unexpected result.

But what really amazed us was this: of the 10 questions, we each only got 4 questions right about each other. However, we had a really awesome time revealing our answers, laughingly arguing about what our favorites *really* were, and how much we did and didn't know about each other after so many years of living together.

So I encourage you to invest an hour on any upcoming "date night" with a Coke and your favorite pizza (Can you agree on this?) to do this little exercise together. It's a great way to begin to make a deposit into each other toward more private quality time at least once a week, getting to know each other all over again. If you feel *really brave* and you have more time, try including some of these additional topics, or ones of your own choice on a second date night:

What's my favorite_____?

Pizza	City
Board Game	Country
Participatory sport	Spectator sport
Place to relax	Place to take a walk
Next vacation spot	Friend

You could even do this at your favorite coffee shop, and all the people there will be envious about the way you seem to be awesomely enjoying each other. Whatever your choice, enjoy! (We played the game sitting up in bed in our jams at bedtime!)

And when it seems we never have enough time, the bottom line is the verse that reads so well in the Modern Language Bible. Ephesians 5:15-17: *"See to it, therefore, that you conduct yourselves carefully, not as foolish but as wise people, who make the best possible use of their time, because these are evil days. Be not thoughtless, then, but gain insight in the Lord's will."*

Ask the Holy Spirit in the days ahead to help you do a running inventory blow by blow, day by day, to see how you're doing in this regard. And I suggest you also consider asking each other (gently) how you're doing as well. And may He give you the grace to be both honest and gracious with each other, making quality time together a higher priority in your life.

Chapter 4

~ TOGETHER ~

"Let us hold unswervingly to the hope we profess, for He who promised is faithful. And let us consider how we may spur one another on toward love and good deeds."

Hebrews 10:23-24

This word "spur" caught my eye, so I looked it up in the Greek, and the word "paroxysmos" means "encouraging or spurring on toward a goal."

The only clear picture of this in my mind's eye is that of "barrel racing" competitions when I was a teen-ager. My earliest memory is falling off of a horse when I was about 3 years old, and I don't ever remember "learning to ride." I just somehow always knew how. My two sisters and I rode the mile and a half to school at Prairie Home, the one-room school house where my father went to grade school, and where years later my mother taught school before I was born. Riding horses was as natural as brushing my teeth, whether with a saddle or bare-back.

There were chores to be done with our horses, such as rounding up cattle to be sprayed or vaccinated, or moving cattle from one pasture to the other. Horses are smart, and if trained well are very responsive to movements of the legs or reigns. Rarely was any real aggressive action needed to get where we wanted to go, and get there fast. It was a part of life on the farm. Oh what invaluable memories!

But when I became a teen-ager we joined the Saddle Club in a nearby town, and on Friday nights we would get together in Pleasanton, (meaning pleasant town) a small town nearby of about 700 people, where they had a riding arena. We joined some of our friends and there we began to train and ride in competitive events: pole bending, barrel racing, etc. It was only then that we began to use spurs.

We could get old "Goldie" to go around the barrels without them, but with them she would go faster, and we did better in the frequent showdeos, where we would compete against riders from the other towns. With spurs on, my sisters and I felt like real "cowgirls." We used spurs to get along faster toward the goal of circling each of three triangularly placed barrels more quickly than the girls from the other towns. The winner got a prize (usually a ribbon), and also a reputation.

In the natural, we had to spur on the horse to win the prize. So in a spiritual sense, what is the prize we should spur one another toward, and how do we do it?

I Corinthians 9:24-25 says, *"Do you not know that in a race all the runners run, but only one gets the prize? Run in such a way as to get the prize. Everyone who competes in the game goes into strict training. They do it to get a crown that will not last; but we do it to get a crown that will last forever."*

In Hebrews 10:24-25 we are encouraged to likewise spur one another on toward love and good deeds, or we could also say it *"toward good deeds motivated by love."* I Corinthians 9:24-25 speaks of the goal as an eternal prize or crown. James 2:26 says, *"As the body without the spirit is dead, so faith without deeds is dead."*

These verses all seem to give us a picture of a concrete faith goal (love and good deeds resulting in an eternal crown). The spurring on towards the goals is an active, aggressive pressing into them, not a nonchalant ambling in the general direction of a possible goal.

The key word here is "together" as in Hebrews 10:24-25 *"...spur one another on towards love and good deeds. Let us not give up meeting together...and all the more as you see the Day approaching."*

Athletes will agree that running by themselves can be invigorating and satisfying, but it's the goal of competition with another towards a prize, that keeps them pressing more consistently into the diligence and practice needed to excel.

There are many ways to experience the "together" necessary to spur one another on towards the goals of a mature, reproducing Christian life – not only for yourself, but also those you will lead to Christ. They will themselves receive that eternal prize or crown, and you will teach them also to win and disciple others in time.

It seems ideal, however, that the one closest to us day in and day out, the one who knows best our strengths and weaknesses, and the one who the most has our best interests at heart should be the ideal "together" partner to spur us on toward the goals and the prize. And the process implies something more than a passive encouraging, but rather an aggressive "spurring on" such as we did with our horses in the barrel races. This seems one of the most unique privileges of marriage, and yet one of the most rewarding. It is a unique laboratory, as it were, conducive to the active molding of a person into the character of Jesus Christ.

I remember Dave and I experienced some primarily blissful first months of marriage, and then we began to experience some quarrels; some sparks began to fly as we noticed that *"iron sharpens iron, so one man sharpens another"* (Proverbs 27:17). At some point we questioned each other why the Lord didn't let some of these more difficult issues come up *before* we got married. Finally, we felt we had an answer from the Lord ... "because you would have run." In other words, had we not been within the binding and lasting covenant of marriage, we might simply have run away from each other as unpleasant sparks began to fly, while God continued to work off the rough edges that were not yet conformed to the character of Jesus Christ.

We became more and more convinced that the "together," safe, loving and lasting laboratory of marriage was the key environment for God to use in gradually conforming us into the likeness of His son Jesus. Romans 12:2 says, *"Do not conform any longer to the patterns of this world, but be transformed by the renewing of your mind ... to test and approve what God's will is..."* Together is God's place for so much more too!

Chapter 5

~ TRANSPARENCY ~

I remember watching my father working in his shop to sharpen each triangular blade making up the sickle that would cut down the hay in the field, so it could be baled for hungry horses and cattle in winter months ahead. I would watch from a distance, and he wore a mask to protect his face and eyes from the sparks that flew wildly from the metal as it was pressed against the moving grinding stone. It fascinated me.

But to this day it reminds me that as *"iron sharpens iron"* sparks will fly, but together they get the job done of forming that cutting edge to pierce the darkness of the enemy's kingdom, setting the captives free and raising up an army for the Kingdom of God in these last days.

We love for our picture of "togetherness" to be that path of flowers, beautiful sunsets and romantic "sweet nothings" exchanged in our intimate interludes. And though these are vital and useful in demonstrating our love for each other, and in procreating our families, the "together" picture is also one of safe and loving confrontation of the issues God has in mind in order to conform us gradually into the image of Jesus, for His pleasure and the progression of His Kingdom on earth.

There are three inter-related attributes that speak to us some of the methods and manners of "going deeper" with God in our relationships, so that as time marches on we become closer to God and also closer to each other. If I myself, my spouse and God are each seen as being at the points of a triangle whose sides are the same length, then the closer my spouse and I move toward God, the closer we will also move toward each other. The key elements of *transparency*, *tough love* and a *teachable heart* are vital to really knowing and respecting each other as best friends. Also, let's be real and honest with God so He can draw us closer to Him in fellowship and character transformation.

I am reminded of an almost forgotten memory of a time we lived in Germany about 30 years ago. At that time there was a custom in weeks prior to the beginning of Lent called "Fasching." It was a time of revelry and partying that satisfied some of the lusts of the flesh prior to the soul-searching and self-denial season of

Lent, which precedes the days of remembering the crucifixion and resurrection of Jesus.

The one most unique memory of this season was the wearing of a costume mask to any of the many parties or dances that were held during this time. The attraction was not only the intrigue of dancing with a stranger (perhaps), but also that you could get away with more "borderline" behavior during those events because no one would know who you really were. This is perhaps an extreme example of the practice of "wearing masks" of one kind or another, and we would often hear tales of marital discord among those who had celebrated liberally during this season.

This practice stands in stark opposition to a frame of mind and attitude that is godly and desirable in a healthy marriage – that is "transparency."

I'm sure we all can think of people we know who seem to wear masks in their relationships with others – never going beyond that superficial conversation at the "weather" level, to go deep into the "heart" issues of disappointments, misplaced hopes, unrealized dreams, and the unrealistic expectations of our lives.

Our Bible story of Adam and Eve reminds us in a visual way of God's best plan for man and wife: that is "naked transparency." They were naked and unashamed, and not embarrassed to behold each other, until sin entered in and birthed lies and hiding into the human condition. Mistrust, isolation, fear and doubt are only a few unwanted guests who can come in to crash the blissful state of naked transparency such as they had enjoyed together with God.

It's so sad to encounter couples who after 20-30 years (or less) of marriage seem to hardly know each other, having long ago put aside even a goal of transparency with each other, having settled for a surface conversation no deeper than, "What did you do today?" If you're in one of those relationships, take hope – God has answers for us all.

I believe God's highest desire is for us to be best friends with our mates. When someone else in our life takes the place of our mate in the "best friend" position, especially someone of the opposite sex, we are in very grave danger of compromising the foundation of our marriage as well as our relationship with God.

The human soul longs for a degree of intimacy in transparency with that person we feel we can really trust. Ideally that person is our spouse, and we need to guard against several murderers of transparency. Here is my "shot" at a few of them.

Critical and condescending attitudes:

Your mate hardly gets through a sentence or two of sharing some intimate experiences and feelings, and you interrupt with a statement of judgment, criticism or unsolicited advice. But on the other hand, if your mate shares an intimate experience, thought or feeling with you, you can encourage more of this intimacy if you listen with sensitivity, trying not to pass judgment or give a lot of unsolicited advice. Expressing understanding without judging is a key to transparent sharing of deep and intimate thoughts, feelings or experiences.

Blabbermouth:

This is an inability to share an intimate thought, opinion or experience without fear that your mate will blab it to the guys at work or the girls at the beauty salon. But confidences kept secret between the two of you are like a "secret password" into places of your hearts where no one else can go, and intimacy and love are enhanced. On the other hand, when there is some realistic concern that the confidence you are sharing may not be kept private between the two of you, it causes you to "close your heart" to each other, as a defense against being hurt in a very vulnerable area. These practices are a slippery path towards almost sure death of the intimacy and transparency you want to foster in your marriage. Think twice before sharing precious intimate things relating to your marriage, even with a close friend.

Needing to have all the answers:
You feel you need to "solve" the intimate situation or problem your mate is sharing with you, before he/she even gets through explaining what's on his/her heart. Your partner wants an interested and loving listener who can share the situation, without your sudden impulse to pass judgment or solve the problem immediately. It can sometimes be helpful to paraphrase back your understanding, "That must have been pretty embarrassing" (frustrating, disappointing, intimidating) and so forth. If you want to share more, you may want to ask permission with a statement like, "That gives me an idea; would you like to hear it?" Ephesians 5:21 says,

"Submit to one another out of reverence for Christ." This is a key to almost any conversation or situation.

Just a little word of wisdom especially to you husbands. It is only natural for you to be the "answer man" or the "fix it man." Indeed, God has created you with the wisdom and desire to be able to "fix things" – things at work, things around the house, and things you encounter in your everyday life. Sometimes these roles are reversed, but most often it is the husband who examines the freezer when the food seems to be thawing. I for one really appreciate this truth, and even relish the fact that "I don't do light-bulbs."

So it often comes natural for you husbands to also try to be the "fix it man" when your wife shares some problem she is experiencing, or some intimate feelings related to it. Please consider that most times, she is not looking for a "fix it man." She is looking for a sensitive heart and a soft shoulder to cry on. She just wants you to hear and understand the situation she is going through, and often doesn't necessarily desire, need, or expect you to have solutions handy for her. When you need to voice your opinion or your solution before she finishes sharing her heart with you, it may cause a "shut down" on your intimate conversation.

Also wives, we really need to try harder to appreciate this God-given trait in our husbands, not taking for granted the many things he does to protect us and make our life easier. We could do well to reward him more often with words of praise and appreciation when he does the dirtier tasks, the ladder jobs, and the flat tires. And we need to be gentle and gracious when we have to remind him more than once that the light bulb in the guest bedroom needs to be changed. A gentle reminder will usually get the job done faster than sharp or sarcastic nagging.

And husbands and wives, it is wise to ask the Holy Spirit to help us "hear ourselves" when we speak to each other. The marriage license is not a license to speak to each other in caustic or hurtful ways that we would never speak to someone else. Just like natural scars on our skin often remain throughout our lives, scars on our hearts from thoughtless, caustic words can remain there to hinder the tender sensitivity we both desire to have towards each other.

The marriage license is a license to remember the words of wisdom in Ephesians 4:29-32: *"Do not let any unwholesome talk come out of your mouths, but only what is helpful for building others up according to their needs, that it may benefit those who listen. And do not grieve the Holy Spirit of God, with whom you were sealed for the day of redemption. Get rid of all bitterness, rage and anger, brawling and slander, along with every form of malice. Be kind and compassionate to one another, forgiving each other, just as in Christ God forgave you."*

Conversely, one difficulty with the tendency of men to be the "fix it man" is that you are often reluctant to share your own concerns, questions and insecurities for fear that it conveys an inadequacy or some form of lack on your part. This need to justify oneself with "being right" with our spouse, our children, or our daily circumstances can prove to defeat us; when what we really need to be is vulnerable, real and transparent with our spouse.

Chapter Six

~ TOUGH LOVE ~

We encounter the need for tough love when we need to share something that may be difficult to receive. An example comes to mind.

You are the parents of a Jr. High student who is starting to play basketball on the school team. One of you gets deeply involved in the action at hand, and loudly shares your opinions with the coach, the ref, or the other parents in an uncontrolled display that is mortifyingly embarrassing to you, and also to your 8th grader.

The "other" parent exhibits "tough love" in privacy together after arriving home. He/she gently shares how this behavior looks and sounds to others and how it is being poorly received by the coach, referee or parents of other children. The point is carefully made of how potentially embarrassing this loud display is to your son or daughter who is doing his/her best to learn to play the game. Perhaps a less inflammatory behavior style could be gently suggested.

Sometimes we live with a certain behavior pattern in our spouses that simply "drives us crazy," without ever investing the time and courage to confront them gently and arrive at a solution or a compromise that's more "user friendly" to you as a couple.

There have been times in our married life when we didn't want to "rock the boat" or get the other person upset, so we didn't say anything about a situation or behavior that was inappropriate, unattractive, and non-productive to a healthy and secure marriage. In time we found out that eventually our communication patterns were getting bogged down to a surface level, and our romance quotient was likewise seriously waning.

We sometimes tolerate things in our spouse that aren't healthy for either of us, rather than taking the time and energy to find and take advantage of the appropriate opportunity to discuss and adequately deal with the situation, habit, or circumstance that is causing friction between us. Especially when the issues at hand are particularly volatile, it is wise to sandwich the discussion between "before" and "after" brief prayer sessions. The Holy Spirit is the best buffer zone to control the spread of an uncontrolled fire that could destroy your unity.

Tough love will risk the confrontation for the sake of enhanced unity and compatibility for the long haul experience of married life together.

We find there are a number of reasons or excuses for why we don't confront difficult issues.

Don't rock the boat:

"I didn't want to rock the boat or get you upset with me, so I didn't say anything." We sometimes tolerate things in our relationship with our spouses that aren't healthy for either of us, rather than taking the risk or effort to tackle the issues appropriately. But in time these relatively small offenses or irritations can grow to be major hindrances to ongoing harmony and unity in your marriage. One way to begin to face these little waves of discord that threaten to sink our boat of harmony and joy is to call a "time out" session between you. This might be on a Saturday morning or other unencumbered period when you can invest a little open-ended time to discuss issues of irritation or disappointment one or both of you are experiencing in your relationship. If you can build this sort of "time out" opportunity into the fabric of your relationship, it will seem less of a threatening crisis to overcome, and will seem more like "routine maintenance" that is required by many precious or expensive pieces of equipment.

This brings to mind the Grandmother clock (a slightly smaller version of the Grandfather clock) that has always stood in the hallway of our house. Somewhere along the way, following a number of moves we have made as a family, the delicate mechanisms got slightly scrambled, and the chimes just couldn't be made to match the hours. We tried, but we couldn't adjust it ourselves, and we simply couldn't tolerate the discrepancy, so we let it sit idle for a number of years. We had many excuses for not getting it fixed, from not being able to find a repair person in our area, to not having the extra cash to make the repairs, to not taking time and energy to haul it to a repair shop. But whatever the reasons, the beautiful clock just stood there with her arms folded and her mouth silent. She travelled with us from move to move, and finally on this last move she never made it to the house from the garage, where other things were stored that didn't quite fit in with the space or décor.

But last year I finally said, "Enough is enough!" I wasn't going to see this lovely and functional item fall apart over time in the damp garage. I invested the time to find a repairman in our area, and together we hoisted the old gal into the back of Dave's pickup for the trip to the town where the repairman had his shop. A couple of weeks later we paid the price for the repair as an anniversary gift to each other, and brought the lady home again to a prominent spot in the living room. A generous application of "Old English" was just the make-up she needed for those aging spots that had developed over the years, and she looks good as new. The watchmaker had said she was of fine quality and should perform well for many more years.

Our marriages are also of infinite value in the sight of God, and in the lives of not only ourselves, but our children, their children, and countless others in our circle of friends and church family. The time it takes to perform "routine maintenance" is worth the investment to enhance day to day function and satisfaction, and to guard against deterioration in the future.

I implore you to find that small section of time that you can set aside routinely for "maintenance" in the form of uninterrupted communication together and with the Lord, in order to bring up some of these delicate issues and make the necessary adjustments for harmony and satisfaction. And if you find the adjustments are simply too complicated for you to make them between yourselves, don't hesitate as long as we did to bring into the picture an experienced worker who could help us make the adjustments we needed in order to save our clock. Your relationship is of far greater value than any clock, and it deserves the maintenance it needs in order to function in the harmony you desire. Today we can enjoy the beautiful and accurate chimes of that clock on an hourly basis, and we're very thankful for our investment.

Rapid defense mechanism:

This little term is one we coined some time back as we worked through one of these routine maintenance sessions together with the Lord. We identified it as one of the major hindrances we had in maintaining the intimacy and harmony we both valued greatly in our marriage.

Let me try to describe how it worked. If one of us would start to discuss a sensitive issue in our interactions together, the other would sometimes create a road-block to going deeper into the problem. We discovered later this was really a defense mechanism designed by our inner man to keep from going into the areas of our memories or personalities that were painful to go into.

The road block was in the form of a "rapid defense mechanism." It operated in such a way that when one would begin to discuss an issue of disharmony or dissatisfaction between us, the other would quickly state in so many words, "It wasn't *me.*" before there could be any real discussion of an issue. It was sort of like Mom asking who emptied the cookie jar thirty minutes before supper. "It wasn't *me*!" We each were quick to pass blame to the other partner, rather than take an honest look at what might be present in our own personality, our bank of experiences and memories, or our own areas of woundedness from either recent or distant past events.

Once the Lord had revealed to us this dysfunctional pattern in our communication with each other, it was not a difficult issue to confront and repair with His help. We both discovered our need to "own up" to our own issues that contribute to a lack of marital unity

77

and harmony. We are learning to confront and solve such personality traits or habits in order to move forward in deeper intimacy and harmony with each other.

But owning up to our needs to make adjustments is sometimes the most difficult part. It is here we need to rely most heavily on the Lord to be faithful to His Word in Hebrews 4:12-13: *"For the Word of God is living and active. Sharper than any double-edged sword, it penetrates even to dividing soul and spirit, joints and marrow. It judges the thoughts and attitudes of the heart. Nothing in all creation is hidden from God's sight. Everything is uncovered and laid bare before the eyes of Him to whom we must give account."*

Tough love is a willingness to work your way through an issue, rather than just ignore it. Here we find that complacency is a great deterrent to the fiery love that we want. Complacency is like a soggy, wet blanket, and an opponent to just about anything that is fiery ... even our love.

Love is not a withholding pattern of silence, or an attitude of "I'll get even with him/her" by holding back our affection, sexual encounters, or conversation. This may be tough, but it is not love. Let's consider again briefly the words Paul shared in Ephesians 4:32 - 5:2: *"Be kind and compassionate (tenderhearted) to one another, forgiving each other, just as in Christ God forgave you. Be imitators of God, therefore, as dearly loved children and live a life of love, just as Christ loved us and gave Himself up for us as a fragrant offering and sacrifice to God."*

I remember the time I slid down the cellar door and got splinters in my back side. Mother was very patient and gentle as she probed with a sewing needle to remove each one of them. My prayer is that we can be as gentle with each other as we seek to discover and dismantle these partially hidden and offensive splinters within our relationships that can hinder our communications and impair our efforts to draw closer together.

Chapter 7

~ TEACHABLE ~

When I think of Timothy, I see the epitome of someone who is teachable. In Acts 16 we see that Paul met Timothy in Derbe on his 2nd missionary journey. Study notes suggest that his earthly father was not a believer, but he had other fathers in the faith, and Acts 16:2 says the brothers at Lystra and Iconium spoke well of him. My Bible study notes suggest that he may have been in his teens when he went on with Paul on his journeys. In 1Timothy 4:12 he is still instructing Timothy, speaking of him as a "young man" about 15 years later.

Near the end of Paul's life after his fourth missionary journey, he is still writing to Timothy. In 2 Timothy 3:1-4 Paul is continuing to instruct him, reminding him of the infinite worth and dependability of the scriptures, and encouraging him with some final points of the why and how of continuing to be a wise and effective teacher and preacher himself.

The tapestry of Timothy's life is woven throughout the remaining chapters of Acts, and in First and Second Timothy. I am thrilled to see the effectiveness of Timothy's life from his youth. I see his teachable character as a disciple was perhaps the most important factor in his usefulness to Paul (and ultimately the Lord) in assisting Paul's ministry, in living an incredibly fruitful life from his discipleship as a young man, and in his apostleship directed towards many other fruitful men, women and churches throughout his life.

In 2 Timothy 2:2 we find a truly precious nugget of instruction in discipleship: *"...the things you have heard me say in the presence of many witnesses, entrust to reliable men who will also be qualified to teach others."* We see here four generations following the pattern of Jesus Christ: Paul – Timothy – reliable men – others. Because Timothy was teachable himself, Paul found him to be a faithful and dependable pattern upon which to build generations of disciples for the Lord Jesus Christ.

At this point I have to look seriously into the mirror and see if the reproduction I'm staring at is a true, faithful and dependable one that I want to see reproduced into the lives of young disciples. Am I still willing to be instructed in the ways of our Lord, and changed by His Word? It seems we're never too old to learn and change as we move forward in life as Jesus' disciples.

"When we think we've arrived, we're probably just stuck in the mud."

This is not an old adage, because I just made it up, but I think it applies to the point I'm trying to make. We see some people, in older years, who think they've "arrived" as the disciple, father, husband, etc. that they want to be, and they become less teachable in the fellowship of the saints, or in the living room with their spouse. Paul's succinct instruction to the Romans in 12:2 expresses his heart on the issue so very well: *"Do not conform any longer to the pattern of this world, but be transformed by the renewing of your mind. Then you will be able to test and approve what God's will is – His good, pleasing and perfect will."*

This chapter goes on to warn believers not to think too highly of themselves, and gives many powerful directives for growing in the knowledge and character of Christ.

It so clearly speaks of the ongoing pilgrimage of the Christian life and mind, being renewed and changed by the scriptures of God's Holy

Word and their consistent and ongoing application into our lives.

James 3:17-18 says, *"But the wisdom that comes from heaven is first of all pure; then peace-loving, considerate, submissive, full of mercy and good fruit, impartial and sincere. Peacemakers who sow in peace raise a harvest of righteousness."*

These two verses are totally "action-packed," displaying much of the "how" of sharing and applying the truth of God's Word with each other as husbands and wives.

Joshua chapter 5 is a tale of how God instructed Joshua to oversee the circumcision of all the men who had just crossed over the Jordan, and were preparing to take the promised land, starting with Jericho. This is "naked transparency" of the flesh in action. As they restored the act of circumcision into their midst, God said, *"Today I have rolled away the reproach of Egypt from you."* Volumes have been written about what this act demonstrated, and what the Lord meant when he said it.

Personally, I believe a part of the reproach was their forced servant-hood under ungodly pagan masters in Egypt. It was the reproach of observing and participating in some measure (even as servants) in the ungodly and unbiblical ways of the Egyptians' life and worship. It was the inability to fully know and carry out the teachings of their faith within their captivity as prisoners and servants in Egypt. It was a rolling off of the shame of the punishment of the 40 years of wanderings in the desert.

It was a beginning of restoration to all of the "Jewishness" as God's chosen people. And we see in Joshua 8:30-35 how he restored an altar to the Lord, and the reading of the Law to the people; including men, women, children and aliens who lived among them.

The bodily circumcision was a formal "rolling-off" of the patterns and ways of Egypt, to enter into the fullness of all God had prepared for them in the promised land.

Dave and I believe with all our hearts that this place of "naked transparency" together as husband and wife in the presence of God, and the instruction, affirmation and encouragement of the scriptures is God's very best place for us to roll off, day by day the thoughts and ways of the "old man" in order to be conformed in our minds, hearts and actions to the character and heart of Christ. "Do not conform any longer to the pattern of this world, but be transformed by the renewing of your mind." Romans 12:2.

Sometimes we hear the old adage spoken, "Your actions speak so loud, I can't hear what you're saying." I wonder if our actions say more than our words about whether or not we are teachable in the things of God and His Word. I never tire of reading the words of Isaiah 50:4-5: *"He wakens me morning by morning, wakens my ear to listen like one being taught ... and I have not been rebellious; I have not drawn back."*

Here is the question at which we arrive as we close this chapter:

"Can we say with the prophet Isaiah that we have been eager to hear what God wants to teach us, and we have not drawn back or neglected that place of instruction that the Holy Spirit is preparing for us day by day?"

No matter how many years we have been married, God wants to continue to teach us how to follow Him more closely in intimate fellowship and discipleship. And within that enhanced fellowship lies the wisdom and grace we need to stir up the coals of our fiery love for each other. The last word is this advice in Hebrews 10:25: *"Let us not give up meeting together as some are in the habit of doing, but let us encourage one another – and all the more as you see the Day approaching."*

Sometimes we tend to look for flaws in the "teacher" in order to find an excuse to not obey the clear teachings of the scripture. Such an attitude of self-justification is dangerous and perhaps even deadly.

Psalms 119:165 says, *"Great peace have those who love your law, and nothing causes them to stumble"* (to be offended). If I love the Word of the Lord, regardless of how it is presented to me, I should not be offended, refusing to consider or obey the admonitions. But I should be willing to embrace the principles and patterns that the Word of God presents for me.

Chapter Eight

~ TALK ~

Talk. It is so fundamental to the strength of our marriages, our lives as husband and wife, as parents and grandparents, as disciples, and as ministers and missionaries that we wrote a small book about it years ago called, *"Meet Me in the Garden in the Morning."* It describes how we can take this atmosphere of being teachable to its highest level of productivity with and for God as we come together morning by morning to read, study, discuss and pray over God's Word before the sun rises and the day starts. It's so awesome to be naked before each other and God in the process, even as Adam and Eve were naked in the garden before the fall, and lived together without shame (Genesis 2:25).

In all our years of married life we have failed only a small handful of times to meet together in this way morning by morning, except in those instances when we were separated by distance. God has been so faithful to us in these times of coming together. And by His grace God has empowered us to use the gold nuggets from His Word and our notes from these morning studies of it as the foundation for a number of the books we have written. And it serves as one of the foundation stones upon which the Lord Jesus has built our lives and our ministry as missionaries.

As we started on our honeymoon to read, discuss His Word and pray together, we could never have even dreamed of what He had in store for our lives as a couple.

So if anyone would ever ask, "What is a primary key to your lives, your marriage and your ministry?" we would quickly answer:

God's Word first, early in the morning day by day, every day, together in His presence ... and the prayer together that applies what we have gleaned in our Bible study and discussion, to our ordinary lives and experiences.

In teaching marriage seminars we usually teach this cute little song, *"Make a mini-manna-muffin for your mama in the mornin' and she'll love ya' all day long!"*

Truly, Christian men, your participation in gathering with your wife the daily manna from God's Word, and making it into something concrete, applicable and nourishing in your lives can serve to be the most useful, attractive and lasting expenditure of your life efforts as you seek to love and serve the wife God gave you.

But what about just talking with each other? What does it look like? What forms does it take in the life of a healthy marriage? We took a few moments to reminisce about some of the times and ways we like most to talk.

Walkin' talk:

- Walking on the beach, talking about the power of God at work in the mighty wind and waves, and His powerful work in our lives.
- Walking through the mall, talking about the styles we see and the variety of people walking the mall with us.
- Walking backward, looking back to review past or recent events in our lives separately or our lives together.
- Walking forward, considering upcoming events and dreaming dreams for the future.
- Walking through the yard, considering what plants or flowers we want to plant.

Driving talk:
- Driving for hundreds of miles, reading and talking about the scriptures and their application to our lives, our marriage and our work.
- Driving to the country café a few miles away for a bowl of soup and a mid-day pause to share thoughts about what we're each working on.
- Building a pattern of talking to each other in the ordinary times, so that at times of crisis or difficulty we have a developed pattern in place.

Sweet Talk
- Sweet talk is a talk of endearments and cutesy little things that are just between the two of us.
- Sweet names we use only for each other that help us to develop a secure sense of identity and endearment.
- Sweet nothings, memories or words no other people can understand.

(I wonder who developed the phrase "My old lady" or "My old man.") Oh my! It should be illegal!

Wonder talk:

- Remembering together some of the "greats" as we walked through the Amsterdam art museum.
- Recounting together the things that take our breath away: a baby's tiny hands or a butterfly.
- Sharing the joy and thrill of moments of beauty such as a sunset, or the coldness of a still afternoon mountain range with its blues and grays, or the stillness of a moonless night.

Word and worship:

- Sharing together our interpretation and appreciation of what God has been doing in our lives.
- Singing or humming a worship song together as we start our morning Bible time with God.
- Recounting together the many things we have to be thankful for.
- Talking about the meanings of the Bible passage we just read.

"Let the Word of Christ dwell in you richly as you teach and admonish one another with all wisdom, and as you sing psalms, hymns and

spiritual songs with gratitude in your hearts to God"

Colossians 3:16

"Speak to one another with psalms, hymns and spiritual songs. Sing and make music in your heart to the Lord, always giving thanks to God the Father for everything, in the name of our Lord Jesus Christ."

Ephesians 5:19-20

Chapter Nine

~ TENDER ~

The dictionary definition of "tender" is: having a soft texture, weak, delicate, expressing or responsive to love or sympathy, loving, compassionate, sensitive, sympathetic, warm, warmhearted.

If "tough love" is on one end of the spectrum, then perhaps "tender" is on the other end, bringing balance to the man and woman of God. The definitions above are from Webster's Dictionary, but let's see what God has to say about it.

Philippians 2:1-2,5,7 says *"If you have any encouragement from being united with Christ, if any comfort from His love, if any fellowship with the spirit, if any tenderness and compassion, then make my joy complete by being like-minded, having the same love, being one in spirit and purpose ... Your attitude should be the same as that of Christ Jesus ... taking the nature of a servant."*

I Peter 3:8: " ... *because of the tender mercy of our God, by which the rising sun will come to us from heaven ...*"

Philippians 4:5: "*Let your gentleness be evident to all. The Lord is near.*"

Ephesians 4:32: "*Be kind and compassionate (NIV tenderhearted) to one another, forgiving each other, just as in Christ God forgave you.*"

It seems to me tenderness comes easier and more naturally to women than it does to men, but I could be wrong. Not only the American culture, but many if not most cultures around the world value common attributes for men of strength, courage, dominance, valor, endurance, aggression, toughness etc.

In many ways these seem an antithesis to tenderness, and "strong men" sometimes find their expected and appreciated traits of such "manliness" to be an excuse for not being "tender."

When I want "tender," I want loving, kind, compassionate, gentle, sensitive, merciful, even romantic. It means to me gentle touches, sweet caresses, careful and patient listening, understanding, forgiving and "filling in" for my weaknesses. It means opening doors, carrying heavy packages, taking my hand over curbs and mud puddles, doing the hard dirty jobs, and a gentle thumb on my cheek when a tear of sadness or regret escapes. It means help with the dishes when there are yet children to bathe and put to bed. It means *him* on the ladder to change the light bulb or hang the picture. It's scraping the snow and ice off the car windows and the heater running before I get there. It means a little more grace on certain days of the month. It looks like a single rose for an anniversary, a loving birthday card, a dinner out on some of these special occasions, or at the least him doing the cooking and dishes one night. It includes taking the dog out to go pee when it's already dark outside; or lighting the fire, taking out the trash or changing a tire.

I like to see the tears that come to his eyes as he comforts someone who is grieving, the squeeze of an uncertain hand, an arm around a tired shoulder – mine or someone else's when necessary and appropriate.

Some of these things will not be at all important to some of you ladies reading this book, but I think the majority can identify with many if not most of these definitions or attributes of tenderness, compassion, mercy, and consideration, honoring us as the "weaker sex."

You men may say these things just aren't in your nature. "I'm not the expressive, tender type." "I didn't grow up in a home where things were done this way." "I never saw my Dad do any of those things. So ... give me a break."

Well, let's see if "you deserve a break today." Let's just read Philippians 2:1-4 again: *"If you have any encouragement from being united with Christ, if any comfort from His love, if any fellowship with the Spirit, if any tenderness or compassion, then make my joy complete by being like-minded, having the same love, being one in spirit and purpose. Do nothing out of selfish ambition or vain conceit, but in humility ... each of you should look not only to your own interests, but also to the interests of others."*

It seems to me the traits we're looking for are all found "in Christ," who stooped down from His lofty position to make Himself nothing, and to become a servant to us all unto death. Verse two says we should be likeminded, having the same love, and being one in Spirit and purpose with Christ.

If He has it all, and He is in us, then His grace for the fruits of tenderness should spring forth through us to others, whether we are men or women. No excuses. How do we get the grace flowing through us to express the tenderness our spouse longs and needs to see in us?

1. Repent of doing things "our way" and being resistant to change.
2. Acknowledge all we need for tenderness and love is in Christ.
3. Ask for a greater filling of His Spirit to manifest His personality in and through us.
4. Repent and turn from the old ways of our behavior that don't please God. (Ephes. 4)
5. Ask questions and "study" our mate to discover what her/his unique desires and expectations are.
6. Begin to gradually put into action what we have discovered.
7. Re-evaluate our "success-rate" with our spouse at regular intervals, so we can make necessary adjustments.

We also need to give our spouses room to grow and change over time. What we each wanted and expected of each other in our 30's may be quite a bit different from what we need and expect in our 50's.

Tears come to my mind as I picture "tender" in its most precious and self-sacrificing living definition.

My mother fought a battle with breast cancer at age 71, thinking she had won. But at 77 it had returned in full force and set up shop in mother's back and pelvis.

Dad had been a farmer, doing all the hard outdoors work of planting and harvesting crops, stacking bales of hay, caring for livestock, and welding or building just about anything that needed to be built.

But now he became the cook, the bottle washer, the washer of clothes, the grocery shopper, the driver and escort to appointments and treatments, and the list grew over the next two years. Their 60th anniversary was celebrated shortly before the end of his opportunities to display his love, faithfulness and dedication – tenderness in all its fullness to the very end.

And surely I have still left the definition and manifestation of "tenderness" inadequately covered in this brief narrative.

Perhaps you'll do better for yourself if you begin your own list of what "tenderness" means, and your spouse can do the same. Knowing each other's answers can make all the difference between your life together manifest as a "bowl of cherries" or an "ashtray of pits."

"Place me like a seal over your heart, like a seal on your arm, for love is as strong as death, its jealousy unyielding as the grave. It burns like blazing fire, like a mighty flame. Many waters cannot quench love; rivers cannot wash it away."

Song of Songs 8:6-7

Tenderness does not only depend upon how we treat each other, but it is also about how we interact with other persons within our frame of reference. If I am thoughtless, rude or crude in my relationship with others, it can diminish or devalue the investment of tenderness I make into my spouse. I may be sharing something with my husband about a friend at my place of employment who is being verbally abused by her husband. I wonder what I would think if my husband were to respond with, "Don't bother me with other people's problems. I have enough problems of my own." This kind of response may equate in my heart to the thought that my husband is not really tenderhearted after all.

Or tenderness can also be measured by how we tend to interact with and discipline our children, or how we usually relate to elderly relatives.

For instance, when a woman sees a husband/father being tender with their children, it opens her heart to be more responsive to him in intimacy, for she sees that their children are being taken care of and treated with loving kindness. But if a man tends to be abusive, abrasive, or even simply "distant" with the children, she will become less responsive with his overtures of intimacy.

Tenderness needs to be more than an activity or action; it needs to be a character attribute that is demonstrated in all the ways we conduct our lives. Just as tough meat is hard to chew and digest, our behavior at times can be pretty hard to swallow. What about you? Are you tenderized?

Chapter Ten

~TRUST~

Proverbs 3:5-7: *"Trust in the Lord with all your heart and lean not on your own understanding; in all your ways acknowledge Him, and he will make your paths straight. Do not be wise in your own eyes..."*

Sometimes when I read a new truth in the scriptures, or in a spiritual teaching from the scriptures, I feel somewhat overwhelmed, not knowing how to even begin to apply the new bites of truth He is feeding me. Then this old friend in Proverbs three reminds me ... one step at a time; one turn at a time and one section at a time.

In my mind's eye I'm in a maze made up of hedges eight feet tall. I can only see the next turn ahead of me and nothing more. Sometimes I am presented with a "T" in the path, and I must go left or right. Which way shall I go?

But now I see myself lifted up by the Lord to a place 25 feet above the maze, and I can see clearly which path to take to make progress through the maze. This vision is such a good reminder that He knows the way through the mazes of our lives, our relationships, our spiritual growth, and our walk with Him. But it is essential that we keep on acknowledging Him each step of the way for every new turn of the path. His lofty vision is comprehensive and long; ours may be only enough to last the next fifteen minutes.

The T's of this small book are most likely not new to you, but perhaps stated from a little different perspective, so you can get a fresh glimpse of your own marriage patterns of loving, respecting, serving, treasuring and pleasing each other. In recognizing some changes you want to make, the faith is released to believe Him for the grace to accomplish those changes in your life and marriage. To echo a motto of my husband, "The grace to accomplish a task is released as you set out to do the task." When God sees that we have a heart's desire to make certain adjustments in our patterns of living married life, He then will release grace (divine enablement) to begin to make them. The first step is to acknowledge your need, and I believe you have begun to do that, simply by taking the time and energy to read this book. God the Holy Spirit is ready to lead you through a new pattern of walking with Him and your mate, which He sees from His divine perspective, and according to His perfect Word.

This takes me to a "life-verse" of mine, Hosea 6:1-3:

"He will heal us ... He will bind up our wounds ... He will restore us, that we may live in His presence. Let us acknowledge the Lord; let us press on to acknowledge Him."

I see here an active partnership in our life walk with God, not a casual ambling along, but an active *pressing on*. I got a life picture of this just yesterday, shopping with my daughter-in-law in an outlet store where there are name brand clothing, household items, and toys at reduced prices. It is early November, and things are not "picked over" by hoards of Christmas shoppers. There were so many aisles to explore and options to consider. How would we manage to check out all the areas we wanted to investigate? We wanted to stay together because it was more fun that way. "Wow, look at this – do you think this would fit in with her kitchen?" So to meet each others' desires to explore certain parts of the store, we had to continually and consciously "acknowledge each other." "What do you think about this?" "Shall we go on to the shoe department?" "Are you finished looking here?"

With all my heart I believe that within these verses in Hosea, and in Proverbs 3:5-6 lies a priceless secret in keeping ourselves in conscious awareness of God's presence throughout the day, pressing into an atmosphere charged with a sensitivity to His personality. And in doing so and obeying His promptings, we are kept on the right path through the aisles and walkways in the challenging maze of life.

My heart's greatest quest and goal is to "acknowledge Him in all my ways," and to demonstrate my love in doing so.

So I am convinced that the application of new ideas or principles you may have gleaned from this simple book will come to you one situation at a time, and one day at a time as you walk with your spouse and God.

To begin to apply some of these points, it will be helpful if you make a brief list of some things you want to work on with God's help and guidance, so that nothing slips through the cracks.

Another secret I've often borrowed from Dave is "mutually reciprocating submission and equality." Sounds like a mouthful of gibberish, but it just means a back and forth exchange (mutually-reciprocating) of submission to each other's desires, goals, preferences, feelings, etc.; keeping in mind that we are equal in God's eyes, and a heavy-handed lording it over each other is not God's desire for us in this partnership of marriage.

As you see God moving and changing attitudes and patterns in your walk with your spouse, you will have grace to trust Him with even more. And He will continue to stoke the flame of the "fiery love" we desire in our marriages.

Chapter Eleven

~TODAY~

Ephesians 5:14-17: *"Wake up O sleeper, rise from the dead, and Christ will shine on you. Be very careful, then, how you live – not as unwise but as wise, making the most of every opportunity ... do not be foolish, but understand what the Lord's will is."*

I'm sitting in my easy chair wondering what I would do with my husband today if I knew it would be our last day together. It's not too different, probably, from what I think the day before I send him out to the other side of the world without me. Usually we go together to the mission field, but this time it didn't work out, so he's just completed a grueling schedule in India, and in Burma (Myanmar) this week. Then on from there for two more weeks of Asia mission points before I see him again. I don't even want to know how many flights there will be until I see him again in Portland.

Speaking of flights, one very memorable flight in particular sticks in my mind. We were in Saigon, Viet Nam and had boarded a flight for Da Nang a couple hours to the North to meet with a mission partner. This was perhaps around 1996.

We boarded the plane, and took our seats. As we looked around we wondered what we had gotten ourselves into. The seats, cushions, and carpet all looked old and worn. Several seats had been ripped out, leaving a gaping hole for several rows, and in another place discarded seats had just been stacked. I had taken Russian for awhile the year before, and recognized the writing on the walls and seat pockets as Russian. It didn't leave us feeling very confident. But we held our ground, and we felt much better in the air. Then about fifteen minutes into the flight, we heard an announcement in Vietnamese and also in English that we were having a problem with the plane, and we would have to return to Saigon. We looked at each other warily and then held hands on the way back.

When the plane came to a stop on the tarmac, we thought we might be deplaned, but no chance. Our window was over the port wing, and soon a ladder was placed near the end of the wing. Our jaws dropped in harmony with each other as we saw two welders brought up on a wheeled ladder so they could reach the point in question on the wing. Then much to our surprise they started welding something there. There were no explanations regarding what was going on, or that we should shield our vision; nor were there any instructions to deplane. I recalled that the fuel for the plane is often stored in the wing, and I felt a cold chill go through my body. We looked at each other, and it was too late to try to deplane. But we did wonder if this could be our last attempt at flight.

Thankfully, it didn't take them long to do the job, whatever it was, and we were taking off again to Da Nang to the North. All's well that ends well, and the flight was uneventful from then on. We've flown many dozens of flights in the past 17 years of mission work, and this is probably the only one we won't ever forget. It's hard to forget something that takes you even close to the thought of death.

We don't really want to think about the possibility of death, either our own, or that of a loved one. If you happen to have a loved one battling cancer, or facing some other potentially fatal illness, you can't really avoid the thought of it, even if you want to.

So, why did I title this chapter "Today?" The reason is so we could take even a few serious moments to consider how we would live life with our spouse if we knew it was our last day together. That is if one of us were to die, or even to face the possibility of death, as one might if saying good-bye to a soldier spouse going off to a war zone somewhere in the earth.

In examining this even briefly I thought of three things right off the bat.

1. Make up.
2. Make love.
3. Make plans.

Since we have no way of looking into the future, we never know what could happen tomorrow, and I believe we should live ready for that possibility. Not in any morbid sense, but merely to live in such a way as to enjoy every day to its fullest and to avoid regrets. Let's examine each point briefly.

MAKE UP: Now, I don't mean the kind you wear on your face. But on second thought, I will take a moment to comment briefly on that. You see I don't look too decent without make-up, and almost never go through a day without it. I try to have my face, hair and clothing all looking presentable to my husband every day. In our times apart, I don't want him to pull up a memory of me without make-up, my hair a mess, in an old T-shirt and ragged jeans. Life with him is a privilege, and every day is as a date to me.

But I really want to talk about the other kind of "Make up." In other words, don't stay upset, angry or otherwise out of sorts with each other. I don't believe God wants us to get out of fellowship with our spouses for even a few hours, let alone for a few days. I think He wants us to live our lives so we are *making the most of every opportunity."* Ephesians 5:16

New King James Version " ...*redeeming the time because the days are evil."*
Modern Language Version "...making the best possible use of their time."
Living Translation "Be careful how you act; these are difficult days."
Revised Standard Version "... making the most of the time..."

Can you think of a time when you lost part of a day or week of your time with your spouse because you were having a disagreement and weren't able to solve it? Neither wanted to give in and claim responsibility for the problem or say, "I'm sorry." Then imagine briefly a scenario where one of you would die in an accident without having a chance to make up from your disagreement? Morbid? Yes, but better safe than sorry. These things do happen.

"The way to live right, is to *live right*"... right with God; and right with each other. Don't let the sun go down on your heated argument. Let the Son rise up in the middle of it and cool things down, with an apology, an explanation, a measure of understanding, or seeing the issues from the other perspective. Live reconciled with each other one moment and one day at a time.

But, you know what? It's not all about you! The Word says this: *"Do not let any unwholesome talk come out of your mouths, but only what is helpful for building others up, according to their needs, that it may benefit those who listen. And do not grieve the Holy Spirit of God, with whom you were sealed for the day of redemption. Get rid of all bitterness, rage and anger, brawling and slander, along with every form of malice. Be kind and compassionate (tenderhearted NKJV) to one another, forgiving each other, just as in Christ God forgave you."*

Ephesians 4: 29-32

We could camp on these verses for a long time, but we're going to pull out the phrase, *"and do not grieve the Holy Spirit of God..."* Some of you reading this book are in Christian ministry, or at least have some responsibility within the Body of Christ, your Christian fellowship, and of course your family.

When you are seriously "at odds" with your spouse and haven't made-up, it grieves the Holy Spirit who has already sealed you up as "one flesh." When the Holy Spirit is grieved, His anointing and grace lifts off for a season, until we make things right with Him and others. The lack of authentic Holy Spirit anointing on you could impact your responsibilities in ministry, in your job, in your role as parents, etc. It's not all about you! The Lord wants you to live right with Him, and also with those people with whom you have relationships and responsibility. Letting yourselves stay out-of-sorts can even have some serious repercussions beyond your husband and wife relationship, so prayerfully consider how you can work out the dynamics of problem solving in your marriage to keep you in harmony with each other. Last of all, remember that formative little lives may be seeing and hearing every word and action. If certain scenarios are repeated often enough, they become imprinted on those little minds and hearts in ways that may spoil the print on the record of their own marriage licenses some years hence.

MAKE LOVE: As a farm girl at heart, the phrase just popped up, "Make hay while the sun shines." It seems to sort of fit this topic.

While we're still in the mind set to consider the "what ifs" of life, what about making love? It seems the older we get, the more weary we become towards evening after a busy day at work, with small children under foot, or older children being driven to sports practices or piano lessons. Sometimes our good ideas in the morning just run out of gas before the sun goes down or the kids are in bed. Does one day run into a week, and a week into two? Soon that God-given "glue" to help cement the integrity of our marriage begins to weaken. Could that ever happen in your marriage?

I remember about 10 years ago a season when Dave and I were busy coordinating some medical and dental clinics in the Philippines, along with the training and evangelistic meetings. There were a lot of preparations to be finished in the process of gathering, categorizing and packing donated medical supplies so they were ready to carry with our team to the mission field. Not to mention the many other things that needed to be made ready at home to go away for a month or two. In this particular season we had a huge amount of preparatory work to do, and Dave was leaving a couple weeks before I would be able to leave my work and join him. So there hadn't been much time for those intimate moments.

We found ourselves down to the last hours, knowing we'd be apart soon. We raced to the airport to check him in on time, and proceeded on to the gate, dreading to say "good-bye" to each other, especially under the circumstances.

And then, suddenly we saw a light in the storm! Just up ahead on a side concourse of the airport was a sign on a door that seemed to beckon like neon: FAMILY RESTROOM. Well, we took a brief pause to be "family" in the private family restroom, and we parted contentedly. "Too much information!" you may say. That may be true, but perhaps some of us married couples need to be more impulsive, more innovative, or at least to make more important in our lives the romantic moments for which we used to find more time.

Just this afternoon I was talking to a young woman who is a very close friend. She is in her mid-30's and married almost 15 years. She told me she had gone shopping yesterday at her favorite department store. When I asked her what she bought, she did not miss a beat in telling me about the professional outfits for her job, and also about several items designed specifically for her "date-times" with her husband. These were the "tight where it looks good," "low cut for only him," and otherwise "for his eyes only" pieces to wear on the special occasions they regularly scheduled without the two kids under six.

Make plans to make love. Or the lack of it may make your marriage vulnerable for failure, or at the very least lukewarm, boring and disappointing. If you would make some special preparations for the last night before your spouse goes away for a long season, why not make any ordinary night (or day) "memorable?"

Use your own imagination!

MAKE PLANS: My Mom and Dad had hired a man with a bulldozer to carve out a section of valley on a piece of their property, and build a dam at the downhill side, creating a four acre lake. I can remember fishing in the lake in the early 50's, when I was a small girl, with my cane pole and bobber. It was a site of picnics for the family on Easter and other special days, and sometimes Mom and Dad would park his truck on the bank and watch the sunset in the West behind the lake. Later, after Mom had passed away, Dad told Dave and me how they had talked about pulling their little Airstream trailer the three miles from their house to this hillside to enjoy the many wild birds, the good fishing, and the soothing water for a few days' rest, here and there amidst the busy farm routine. Dad was a little sad that they never actually did it, though thankfully they did make several good trips a year with their camping trailer to Bennett Springs in Missouri for fishing and relaxation.

Dave commented to Dad what a beautiful site it would be to build a home. As a carpenter and builder he was always seeing such things. Dad said, "Why don't you build a house here then?" To make a long story short, we did just that. Dad willed me a small piece of land early, and within a year of Mother's death we were well on our way in the construction of our new home on the site where Mom and Dad had dreamed of parking their camping trailer. Having lived much of our lives in the Tacoma – Seattle area of Washington State, we took seven years off and moved to Kansas, where Dad, then in his 80's, helped us with some of the light work of building our house, and generally supervised the job site day by day. I think it was a major part of his recovery from the loss, grief and loneliness following Mother's death after 60 years of marriage. And we have such great memories of sharing his last years with him.

Now we're at home again in Washington State, near all of our kids and grandkids, and the lovely home in Kansas has been used for a retreat center for several Christian ministries based in Kansas City. This is a rather poignant story with a happy ending. Dad got to enjoy his lakeside view for many family dinners, 4th of July picnics with fireworks over the water, and birthday and Christmas celebrations. God gave him *"exceedingly abundant beyond all you can ask or think..."* (Ephesians 3:20). But sometimes endings aren't so happy. The things we fail to plan can turn out to be a source of great heartache, sorrow or regret at some point in our lives. There's an old saying that says, "If you fail to plan, you can *plan to fail.*" Now is as good a time as any to suggest you plan a couple of hours together "making plans," or at the very least, starting to dream dreams.

This time should begin with a brief look back to remember the "good stuff" you've already experienced together in your marriage. And then take some time to consider where your life is going and where you want to be in the next 10, 20 or 30 years still ahead of you. What life experiences are most important to each of you? Consider how many of your dreams are shared in common. Which ones are important to pursue, and which are not so important?

Life is too short for "I've always wanted to ..." I encourage you to take a date night, a vacation time, or a rainy Saturday to sit down with a cup of hot coffee or chocolate and dream a little together. Regret is often a very hard pill to swallow, or a debt you cannot pay back. Take a few hours to compare notes on your hopes and dreams, to see if there is a goal you might want to reach for together before it's too late.

I remember how Mom and Dad saved our pennies so we could drive to Seattle from Kansas for the World's Fair in 1962. We had an awesome time: my folks, two sisters and me, and the rat terrier packed into our Ford station wagon. We all remember it warmly. I'm so glad they had the vision and ambition to make it happen.

It was life-changing for us in one very unique and wonderful way. Dad had smoked filter free Camels for a number of years, about two packs every day. When we went through the Science Center at the Seattle World's Fair, there was an exhibit demonstrating the effects of smoking on the human lung. I can remember clearly seeing that nearly black pickled lung in the large glass bottle. It sickened my stomach, but it changed Dad's heart. He walked out of that building and never smoked another cigarette. Lung cancer did eventually catch up with him, but not until 45 years later when he was 92, and we had many wonderful years in between.

I think it was life-changing for me also. Had I not gone to see this gorgeous part of the United States, I might not be snuggled today amidst a forest of seventy foot high evergreen trees in our back yard about 100 miles south of Seattle. Perhaps a plan well thought out will change the course of your marriage and family life for the better, too.

I just have to share one more story before I leave this section on making plans. Back in the late 70's we were stationed in the Army in Germany. Mom and Dad came to visit during those three years, and we visited some sights around Germany. Dad's ancestors were from France and his family name came from "Le Sure" (the sure, steadfast) in French. Later in America it was changed to Leasure. He told us years later that he had so wished he had taken a trip to France, especially Paris during his short time with us in Germany.

So Dave took the old bull by the horns and said, "It's not too late; let's go now!" And Dad, being 88 at the time said, "Oh I could never manage that. I'm too old; I wouldn't know how." After navigating parts of Asia for years, Dave and I knew Paris would be a cinch, so Dad agreed to let us be his tour guides to Paris. Mom had been gone for several years and Dad now had a lady friend. So with Dad's permission, Dave called her and asked her to have a special birthday lunch with us for Dad in Montmartre. She said she didn't recognize the place, but she'd love to go. Only then did he tell her the lunch would be in a special section of Paris! So we did go to Paris, just the four of us, and on Dad's 89th birthday we took a boat ride on the Seine River in the shadow of the Eiffel Tower, where over 100 passengers sang "Happy Birthday" to Dad in five languages. I believe it was one of the happiest days in his later life, and he never missed the money he spent taking us to Paris.

All this said just to say, "Don't waste time **not** making plans!" Life is too short for "what ifs." Seek your hearts together with the Lord in prayer. You'll never know what dreams may materialize until you dream them. A close friend of ours in her 70's just returned from her 5th mission trip to Papua New Guinea following her retirement from a lifetime of working at Sears. Life and God are full of surprises. Today is the first day of the rest of your life!

Chapter Twelve

~TURKEY~

Turkey – you've got to be kidding! What in the world does *that* have to do with marital love and compatibility? Let me explain.

In "talkin' turkey" I'm assuming some of you readers are newlyweds or perhaps even engaged and preparing to marry. This issue of how to blend the his/hers preferences into the two most widely celebrated (with turkey) holidays bears at least a short discussion.

There are so many things to be considered in the expectations of not only the two of you, but also of your parents and extended families. And it becomes even more complicated if there has been a death of a parent, or a divorce and remarriage. Now there's another parent who should also be considered. And if by chance it's a second marriage for one or both or you, there may be even other important family members to consider before the last carol is sung and the last bowl of turkey soup is finally fed to the dog.

Three keys to having a happy holiday season are:

1. Expectation
2. Communication
3. Consideration

I remember well the first Thanksgiving together at our new (to us) house. I was very consumed with the task of trying to juggle the turkey and all the trimmings, so they would all land on the table at the same time. And to put another fly in the ointment (how did the first one get there, anyway I wonder?) a single friend of ours came to the door unexpectedly and parked himself in the kitchen chair to chat. Dave and I hadn't discussed the issue that Janice just can't get it all together when folks are visiting and expecting a pleasant, coherent and even festive conversation when she is trying to think, "Now did I add the salt to the gravy yet or not?" Dave didn't realize that even though the gravy wasn't boiling yet, I was! Finally they noticed that I wasn't being a very active conversation partner at the moment, and moved their conversation on into the living room.

But by now I was getting more rattled as the hour neared for the family to start arriving. So I gave Dave the task of setting the table for me, and I turned my full attention toward getting all the items to finish cooking at the same time. Nearer to arrival time when I took a brief moment to check on his progress in the dining room, I took one look at the table and I just *lost it*! Having not clearly voiced my expectation that we would use the "good" china and glassware, he had already set the table with the "everyday" items he was most familiar and comfortable with. I was aghast! Didn't he remember that we *must* use the best dishes, glasses and flatware for Thanksgiving and Christmas?! It was a little late to find it out, but I voiced my dissatisfaction in an inappropriately emphatic fashion, while he tucked his tail between his legs to comply as quickly as possible before the doorbell started to ring.

The tone of our communication and holiday spirit was certainly turned upside down by our utter failure to communicate some of our personal expectations, and to also consider each other's most important issues. In this way we could have arrived at a compromise agreeable to each other, brightening the day.

We did eventually get these issues settled amiably, and subsequent holiday dinners and celebrations are among our most pleasant memories over the years.

But for some of you, even after a number of years together, your family holiday or birthday celebrations can become a point of frequent contention between you.

So remember to grab a cup of egg-nog or spiced cider early in the holiday season, and have a little talk. Where have you "missed it" in the past and failed to meet the expectations of both of you or other family members? And when have you hit the nail on the head for a exceptionally good time?

The issues can get even more complicated when we consider how much money you each have in mind to spend on the culinary delights and the gift for Aunt Susie who already has everything. Communication is a vital key to transforming the *harried holiday headache* into a *happy "Hallmark" hologram* whose warm memories last for many years.

Incidentally, a couple of months ago I sent my sister a picture I had discovered among some old keepsakes. It was of her and Dad in Mom and Dad's kitchen. She had just carved the turkey and was popping a bite of turkey into his mouth for a "taster's test" before it went to the dining table. I had caught them by surprise with the bite in mid-air and it became quite a wonderful memory-bite to be savored for generations to come.

The moral of this story is a clear one. Effective communication of our expectations, with the patience and loving consideration of each other's opinions and desires can stoke the fire for a warm blaze of love during these special times of our lives.

And failing to communicate this way can throw a cold rag on everything, including the master bed.

Chapter Thirteen

~TRUTH~

"Now that you have purified yourselves by obeying the **truth** *so that you have sincere* **love** *for your brothers,* **love** *one another deeply..."*   1 Peter 1:22

~

"The man who says, 'I know Him," but does not do what he commands is a liar and the **truth** *is not in Him.   But if anyone obeys His Word, God's* **love** *is truly made complete in Him.*   1 John 2:4

~

"Husbands, **love** *your wives, just as Christ* **loved** *the Church and gave Himself up for her to make her holy, cleansing her by the washing with water through the Word (of* **truth**)."*   Ephesians 5:25

~

"Do your best to present yourself to God as one approved, a workman who ... correctly handles the **Word of truth**."*   2 Timothy 2:15

~

"Then we will no longer be infants, tossed back and forth by the waves. Instead, speaking the **truth in love,** *we will in all things grow up into Him who is the head, that is Christ."*   Ephesians 4:14

From a myriad of scriptures I looked over, I chose these five for their content, describing God's Word as truth; and 4 of the 5 passages link **loving** one's brother or spouse with **loving** or obeying God and the **truth of His Word.**

Knowing and speaking the truth are a very high priority among the first apostles and disciples who wrote the scriptures.

I feel it's so important to put our time with God in His Word, the Truth, first in our days, guarding it from other obligations that could eat up our time and leave us without the spiritual nourishment we need to start the day and live it well all the way through.

Whether it's oatmeal, Chex, or simply toast and juice, having breakfast gives us energy and brain food for the physical and mental tasks of the day.

I tend to get busy with the things on my "to do" list, and sometimes don't realize I've passed lunch time by an hour or more. Then I start to feel it. One of the first things I notice is that I just can't seem to think or reason very clearly. Sometimes I even feel a little weak or faint. I recognize this as a little episode of low blood sugar (glucose). I grab a piece of fruit or a glass of juice, and then I am restored and I make some lunch. I try to watch the clock more closely next time.

I think we're too often that way with our spiritual food, the Word of truth. When we leave it out of our morning time we often are "high and dry" by noon, without the spiritual boost we need to handle a challenging situation at work, or give an appropriate word of encouragement to a friend or colleague.

One set of verses describes to us most clearly the value of feeding regularly on God's truth in His Word.

Isaiah 50:4-5 says, *"The sovereign Lord has given me an instructed tongue, to know the Word that sustains the weary. He wakens me morning by morning, wakens my ear to listen like one being taught. The sovereign Lord has opened my ears and I have not been rebellious; I have not drawn back."*

This passage describes the pattern of God waking us in the morning and opening our spiritual ears to hear and learn what He wants to say to us. He wants us to listen with a readiness to be taught a new nugget of truth for living our own lives, and for ministering to someone else throughout the day. It says He *"opens our ears"* to be on the alert to hear His still small voice of instruction or encouragement. Then He gives us the *"word that sustains the weary."* I think God means he wants us to be ready to receive a word that He has for us to give to someone else who has a particular need: perhaps encouragement when they are discouraged, comfort if they are mourning, hope when they feel like they are failing, or appreciation when they feel no one notices their hard work or special extras they do. These are only examples of how God wants to give us something from His heart that we who wear skin (flesh and bones, able to talk and hug) can deliver *in the natural* to others who need His touch. The scripture says, *"...I have not been rebellious; I have not drawn back."* Isaiah 50:5

How often do we have good intentions the night before, but when the alarm rings we hit it, turning it off and once again turning our backs upon our time in His Word, and the plans He has to use us as His hands and feet that day? This is a subtle form of *turning our backs on God.* I think He must wonder, "When, oh when will they *ever* grow up?"

I believe that's part of why He partners us together with like-minded people who can encourage each other to embrace the discipline to feed upon God's Word, His truth, regularly so we don't have that spiritually-weak spell mid-day, or turn up empty-handed and hard-hearted later in the day when a needy person crosses our path.

The season before you marry is the best time to talk about how to work that vital time with God and His Word into your day together every day. Or even better if you're very serious about each other or engaged to be married, it's a good time to practice the discipline of sharing God's Word together daily.

However, we don't usually recommend this for people in a casual relationship. You might be wondering why. Because this practice requires and encourages an intimate sharing of spiritual thoughts and truths from the deep parts of our soul, and binds us together in intimate and unique ways. If you haven't yet made a decision with God that you want to be headed in the direction of marriage, this kind of spiritual intimacy may be out of season, and could cause you to get the "cart before the horse", so to speak.

Some people say this spiritual intimacy helps spark the fire of desire for physical intimacy as well. And this candle is best not lit until the marriage bed is in sight. So move with caution in this arena.

A morning time with the Lord had been my established routine long before I began to get better acquainted with Dave, as it was also for him. I as a writer loved to write down a few sentences of comments regarding the Bible passages I had read that morning, and what I thought God was saying to me about applying it into my life.

I had access to a copy machine, so I would often copy those few pages from my note-book and send them in the mail (no email back then!) to Dave, 72 miles away. In the evenings we would talk on the phone about these things. Our love for each other and for God grew simultaneously in the months before we were married, so it was only natural to continue the practice of meeting early morning together with God and His Word every day after we were wed. It is our life-line to Him and each other; we have found our lives are not complete without it.

Yes, I realize I've mentioned this concept before, but it is the *"pearl of great price"* in this book and worth repeating so you don't miss my encouragement for you to undertake the one habit that could make or break your marriage.

When the fire is stoked regularly without fail, it doesn't go out amidst the multiple showers of challenges and trials we undergo in life.

Chapter 14

~TENACITY~

A dictionary definition of tenacity is "tenacious, not easily pulled apart, cohesive, tough, holding fast."

We've heard it said of people sometimes, "She has a tenacious spirit." Or, "I like his tenacity in this difficult job."

It's an admirable quality of "sticking in there," or "holding fast" to that which is valuable or meaningful to you. When it comes to marriage, it is pretty much summed up with the closing comments at many marriage ceremonies: *"Now whom God has joined together, let no man put asunder."*

Asunder means: "into separate pieces or separated in position from each other."

With today's divorce rates, I often wonder if most people even have a goal of staying together for a lifetime. But certainly in the Christian marriage it should be the goal.

It has been said that out of our awareness of a thing comes our attitude towards it, and from that springs the action we take. For instance, if we become aware through a TV broadcast that a tornado is approaching, our attitude will be one of serious concern for our life and welfare, and our action will take us to the storm cellar or the next county as fast as we can drive! (Or...to our knees in prayer in the safest place of the house.)

This actually happened once when we lived in Kansas. We were in the middle of our Wednesday evening prayer meeting at our country church. We got a call from a friend in the town 8 miles to the west of us that a tornado had just passed through, doing some damage to properties ... and it was coming directly our way! We didn't waste any time getting in our car and driving quickly in another direction the 12 miles back to our home, where we spent some time in the basement until the storm passed over.

Likewise, if we know the storms of life may seriously challenge our marriages, we may want to take some action. If we become aware that nearly half of marriages in America end in divorce, we may develop an attitude of tenacious desire to avoid being one of those statistics. And our action will reflect an aggressive attitude to nurture our marriage relationship, and seek to correct or oppose any and all forces that stand in the way of keeping our marriage strong and happy.

We will strive to develop a tenacious attitude to protect, guard and nurture our marriage as a high priority in life, not only for our sake, but for the sake of generations yet to come.

The enemy has come to *steal, kill and destroy*, but Jesus resides in us to give us *"life, and life more abundantly."*   John 10:10

Our marriages are the incubators and the training ground for the next generation of believers as disciples upon the earth, and I believe it will be that generation who will usher in the King, our Lord Jesus Christ to planet earth again.

A few hours' drive west from where we live now, is the Lewis and Clark State Park, where there is a memorial to these tenacious pioneers who journeyed from the center of our continent (present day Kansas City) to the far Northwest corner – across the plains, the Rockies, and unbelievably treacherous terrains to reach their destination – the Pacific Ocean that they believed was "out there somewhere." There in this museum is a mock-up of the canoes, hewn out of logs, in which they travelled the last leg of the adventure down the Columbia River with their Native American guide Sacagawea. We also have a video in which this historic adventure is portrayed by actors. And as we now live in Lewis County, Washington, it seems somehow a part of our own heritage. As a matter of fact, only two miles from our home is a small state park also bearing the name of Lewis and Clark.

The piece of land given me in Kansas by my Dad in 2000 is just across the dirt road from the 120 acres that were homesteaded by my Great-grandpa Zebediah Leasure in 1855. Just this week I began to reorganize my grouping of family photographs on the dining room wall. The most prominent is the large antique tin-type photo of Great-Grandpa and Great-Grandma Leasure, who came from the region of Ohio and finally parked their covered wagon at the site where they then homesteaded, about 70 miles southwest of Westport (now Kansas City). It stands proudly on our wall as a monument in our own home of those brave pioneers.

The future five generations of pictures cascade below them on the wall. Grand-parents, our parents, myself and Dave, our children and our grandchildren make up a monument to God's faithfulness. And not far away on an opposite wall is a wooden stand bearing one of our most prized possessions: the huge Bible carried by my Great-Grandpa Zebediah and Elizabeth in their covered wagon as they came from Ohio to Kansas, finally displayed 156 years later on the West coast, an hour from the Pacific Ocean. The generations to follow, by the immense faithfulness of God, have followed their lead in knowing Jesus as Savior and Lord. Here is a visible legacy of their faithfulness and tenacity, a reminder to me that what we do now really does affect the future generations.

In our "you deserve a break today" generation, we are often unmindful of the impact our actions could have on the future generations who follow. As you consider what degree of "tenacious" you are willing or able to foster regarding your own marriage and family, don't neglect to consider carefully the potential repercussions if you do or don't hold fast to the covenant you made with God and your spouse to remain faithful " 'til death do us part."

As I write these last pages of this small book, I consider the preparations I will make to fly out to Montana early tomorrow morning, where Dave's Dad lies not many days from death. Dave is cutting his ministry time a little short in the Philippines, so that God willing he will be able to say his "good-byes" to his Dad in person. And then at 61 Dave will soon become the patriarch of his immediate family.

I ponder Dave's mom's tenacity to drive Dad the 70+ miles to the hospital twice a week for his dialysis for the past 2 ½ years, and I don't want to venture how lonely this *"valley of the shadow of death"* would have been for him without her as his helpmate during this very difficult time. We will each face our own valley, unless Jesus comes back first.

As Dave and I have spent our time, energy and resources these past nearly 20 years in the mission fields of almost 20 countries, we have sought to demonstrate the truth we hold most dear to our hearts. That is the truth that within the living person of Jesus Christ lays the only source for the power we need to live lives of true love and sacrifice for one another.

And in Him alone lies the only promise and reality of eternal life. If you have received Jesus Christ into your heart and life as savior, the one who suffered and died on the cross to pay the price of the consequences for your sin, so you could know His presence now and the promise of eternal life in the future ... that is awesome indeed.

But too often we forget that within the Savior's purchase for us lies a contract of willing submission to His lordship of our lives.

Too often many of the hurdles we face in life are due to our reluctance to give Him the steering wheel to the ship of our lives, so He can steer us to safe water – both in our personal lives, our careers, our marriages, and our impact on the generations birthed through us.

Here is a part of the contract that he signed for us in blood – the blood of His fiery love for us: Isaiah 53:4-5: *"Surely He took up our infirmities and carried our sorrows, yet we considered Him stricken by God, smitten by Him and afflicted. But He was pierced for our transgressions, He was crushed for our iniquities; the punishment that brought us peace was upon Him, and by His wounds we are healed."*

From one who knew the stabbing fire of each lash of the whips upon His back, the un-imaginable suffering on the cross, and the dark cold of death and the grave – from Him and His resurrection alone will come the "dunamis" (dynamite) power to live with a blazing torch of love in a sacrificial manner for our mates.

Even many waters of adversity in our lives cannot wash that blazing torch of love away. **This "fiery love"** will remain, by His sustaining power and grace.

"Place me like a seal over your heart, like a seal on your arm; for love is as strong as death, its jealousy unyielding as the grave.

*It **burns like blazing fire**, like a mighty flame. Many waters cannot quench love; rivers cannot wash it away. If one were to give all the wealth of his house for love, it would be utterly scorned."*

Song of Songs 8:6-7

I invite you to renew your covenant of love and devotion to Jesus today, for from that blaze will come all you need for the torch that lights your life and marriage.

"Lord Jesus, today I renew my covenant of devotion to you as my Savior, receiving your suffering on the cross and death – to pay the price for my sins and sinful nature. And I commit myself anew to you as Lord of my life. I give you permission and ask you to reign in every area of my life: my marriage, my family, my occupation, my relationships and all my dreams and aspirations.

With your flame of fiery love, light and renew again the fire of my love for you first, and then for my spouse. From that love, make our life and marriage a joy and strong sustaining force, for us and our entire household and family.

In Jesus' Name, Amen."

ABOUT THE AUTHOR

Janice Woodrum received Jesus Christ as Lord and Savior in 1972, and experienced revival and re-dedication of her life to a deeper walk with the Lord in 1987. She went forward to the altar of a Sutera Brothers' crusade in Tacoma, Washington in January of 1991, laying down her life for full time service to the Lord Jesus Christ at whatever time He would make such a ministry opportunity possible.

In His infinite wisdom, He chose to open up new avenues of ministry within her local Church body and community first, and beyond that to the foreign fields in Korea and the Philippines in 1994. Doors for Janice and her husband, Dave, have continued to open as their international mission organization, Harvest of Jubilee Groups, International, has spread out into fields including Vietnam, Cambodia, England, India, Pakistan, Nepal, Myanmar, Lebanon, and Zimbabwe.

Their church planting efforts, especially in the under-developed areas of India and Pakistan, have led to the need for solid Biblical training. This precipitated the opportunity for them to create and establish an Associate Degree Bible and Christian Ministry program, currently used at their mission points in many of the ministry countries mentioned above.

Writing and teaching are two of their God-given

gifts, and these have served them well in developing classes and teaching in these Bible schools and the Church at large, in both domestic and international fields – and also in the writing of other books and teachings for edification of the Body of Christ.

Finally, in 2007 Janice was able to retire from a thirty-five year nursing career in answer to her prayer of 1991, moving into full time work with the mission organization, as well as continuing her love of writing, editing and publishing. Janice has Bachelor of Science in Nursing, and Master of Ministry Degrees.

Harvest of Jubilee Groups, International helps to conduct Ministry and Missions Training programs in Washington State and in several other states. They plan, supervise and conduct several short-term mission opportunities in foreign fields yearly. And they provide ongoing apostolic oversight, mentoring and instruction in mission points and Bible schools in most of the above mentioned countries of Asia and Africa.

They are available as stateside speakers for leadership or mission conferences on an ongoing basis.

Harvest of Jubilee Groups, International
411 Zandecki Rd., Chehalis, Washington, USA 98532
hojspm@juno.com
360-262-3027

Other books offered by PTW PUBLISHERS

Hope to Hear Soon: (Longing and learning to hear the voice of God's heart in the best of times and the worst of times) by Janice Woodrum $8.95

Cherish Life, A Biography of Sarah Palin and Family by Janice Woodrum $ 9.95

Bridging Two Worlds: Communicating God's Heart in Today's World (A handbook on the function and operation of prophetic ministry in the Church) by Dave Woodrum

$13.95

"Meet Me in the Garden in the Morning" (A guide to deep marital intimacy with God in the Mornings) by Janice and Dave Woodrum $3.95

The Church Triumphant at the End of the Age (A comprehensive reference of Church history, revivals and restorations, Church today, and finishing the great harvest before the Lord's return) by Nate Krupp and Janice Woodrum $16.95

The Current Global Reformation and its Effect on the World Missions Movement: (A close look at today's radical paradigm shift back to N.T. Church life and missions) by Dave and Janice Woodrum $10.95

Imitate Me as I Also Imitate Christ: (A Study of Intense Discipleship) by Dave Woodrum $10.95

PREPARING THE WAY PUBLISHERS
ptwpublish@q.com,
www.ptwpublish.com

As I think about *"This Fiery Love,"* all I see is us ...
Not looking like we did back then – the cover flatters us!
What I see now in you and me grows deep and stronger ever.
Our love has grown and prospered through sun and stormy weather.
We cannot count the miles we've gone
To share the love He gives us.
We trace our many memories ...
And we gasp at how He's graced us!
But whether there, or here at home,
Our love grows ever stronger.
And on this day we celebrate,
We pray for *"longer ... longer!*

More days to meet before the dawn
To greet the day You've made,
And seek the wisdom of Your heart
Before the shadows fade

Days to work and play and teach and pray
Just doing what we're made for!
And as we do we'll oft see You...
The Great Treasure we adore."

This love is deep. This love is strong.
It *"burns like blazing fire."*
The storms of life can't dampen
Our growing deep desire.

So as we start another year
We draw to Him the nearer.
As we see Him as He really is
We see ourselves the clearer.
May His love be perfected
As we run the race marked out,
Until we rise to meet His face
Still hand in hand so stout.
A thousand years await us; and may we never tire ... with love and trust and
patience, to stoke this growing *FIRE!*   (Wedding Anniversary, January 2011)

157

Lebanon, 2010

ABOUT THE COVER

The photographs for this cover were provided by Amber Woodrum, with cover design by Steven Woodrum. Thank you both for providing the fiery ambiance for this book. Many thanks go to Rebecca EuDaly for providing editing services.

The back cover photo lacks human hands or an image in the photograph placed atop the fireplace, in order to provide a visual invitation for couples to sit down with the Lord for their own "fireside chats."